Gerald Newman

## About the author

Gerald Newman is a solicitor and established trainer on web site topics. He was Deputy Director of Communications at the Law Society, where he ran www.lawsociety.org.uk, a web site attracting 2 million hits monthly. He also created www.solicitors-online.com and has worked with internet developers www.readingroom.net. He conducts successful internet seminars and workshops, and can be contacted at gerald@geraldnewman.com.

## Acknowledgements

Parts of this work previously appeared in *Finance FactFinder* published by Gee Publishing Ltd, and is reproduced with permission. All of the web site images are produced by kind permission of the web sites concerned.

LAWPACK

76-89 Alscot Road London SE1 3AW
www.lawpack.co.uk

ISBN 1 902646 75 4

# Table of contents

**1 Introduction**
- How this book will help you ...................................................3
- Fourteen steps to successful web site marketing ......................4
- Internet: the basics...............................................................8
- What is the future for marketing online? .............................12

**2 Strategy and Planning**
- Step 1: Where are you now? Auditing your position..............17
- Step 2: Where do you want to be? Defining your goals .........21
- Step 3: Who is your audience? Market segmentation............28
- Step 4: How do you get where you want to be?
  Writing your marketing objectives ...........................34

**3 Your Marketing Mix**
- Step 5: Planning your content and services...........................39
- Step 6: People .....................................................................58
- Step 7: Resources ................................................................64
- Step 8: Choosing a domain name. .......................................70
- Step 9: Marketing technology..............................................79
- Step 10: Designing the site ..................................................88
- Step 11: Risk management ...................................................96
- Step 12: Promotion and communication .............................103
- Step 13: Keeping the site up to date ...................................129
- Step 14: Monitoring and evaluating the site: continuous
  improvement.........................................................130

**Appendices** ................................................................................135

**Index**.........................................................................................147

# Part 1

Introduction

# Part 1

## Introduction

### Summary

- Three golden rules and our 14 steps will help you avoid pitfalls and maximise your web site marketing impact

- Use practical ideas to apply marketing theory to the web

- There are plenty of free or low cost resources to help you with internet marketing

- Take stock of the prospects for ecommerce

## How this book will help you

### Making the most of the online marketplace

The internet is ideal for delivering services, selling products and for building relationships with customers. But with sites proliferating daily, how can you make sure your site gets noticed? Is your web site marketing you, or are you marketing it? This book will give you practical new ideas on:

- Marketing strategy.

- Researching the net and finding the best web sites.

- Writing good copy.

- Designing a home page that will grab attention.

- Making a success of ecommerce.

- Selling your project internally.

- Choosing a good domain name

- Search engines - how to get them on your side.

Fourteen steps will guide you through planning and implementing cost effective web site marketing and provide a framework for writing your marketing plan.

## Three golden rules

There are three golden rules for effective web site marketing:

- Make the needs and expectations of your visitors the starting point for your web site. Focus on the benefits your products or services, and your web site, will provide to users and customers. Don't focus on descriptions of your product or service.

- Build marketing into the web site from the beginning. Promotion won't be effective if bolted on as an afterthought; your site's design, content and the way customers can use it to communicate with you should all be planned with the marketplace in mind.

- Content is king. How can your web site help customers tackle problems or improve their daily lives? If your web site doesn't offer something worthwhile, people won't visit it.

This book's 14 step guide will help you apply these key principles.

## Fourteen steps to successful web site marketing

The 14 steps are:

1. Where are you now? Auditing your position. Getting familiar with the internet. How to find statistics, information and training. Which web sites can you learn from?

2. Where do you want to be? Defining your goals. What do you expect your firm, and visitors, to gain from your internet site?

3. Who will be your audience? Market segmentation. How to choose a focus for your site.

4. How will you get from where you are now to where you want to be? Writing your action plan.

5. Plan your content and services: Which of the six internet site models is best for you: brochure material, content-rich, interactive, ecommerce enabled, the virtual business, an extranet?

6. People: How to get internal buy-in.

7. Resources: Where to get help to implement your site. Choosing and using PR consultants.

8. Your domain name: How to choose and protect your online brand name.

9. Technology: Why you should think twice about using frames or flash animation.

10. Design and branding: What makes a good home page?

11. Risk management: Testing your site. Ensuring legal compliance.

12. Promotion and communication: Includes tips on internet search engines.

13. Keeping the site up to date.

14. Monitoring, evaluation and continual improvement.

You can write a marketing plan by recording your choices, actions and plans, in relation to each of these headings. Promotion activity itself (Step 12) is only one part of the picture. Marketing has a much wider definition, because so many other factors contribute to how your product or service will fare in the marketplace.

# Marketing basics

## Practical - not theoretical

Our approach to marketing is intended to be practical, so we have avoided academic discussion of marketing theory. But you will find the following topics covered:

- We define marketing, and explain the 'marketing mix' (Product, Price, Place, Promotion, People and Processes) in this section of the book.

- Branding is discussed in Step 2 - defining your goals.

- Market segmentation, product life-cycles and relationship marketing are dealt with in Step 3 - defining your audience.

- Relationship marketing is explained in Step 5 - choosing your content and services.

# What counts as marketing?

The Chartered Institute of Marketing defines marketing as:

> The management process of anticipating, identifying, and satisfying customer requirements profitably.

The width of this definition is deliberate. Marketing is much more than simply promotion activity, and includes:

- Analysing your market and your customers' needs.

- Predicting and monitoring how these might change and develop.

- Designing products or services that match your resources and skills to the market.

- Ensuring you meet your own goals for your business as well as satisfying customer expectations.

What goes into this wide-ranging marketing mix and how does it apply to your web site?

## The marketing mix: the '4Ps' and more

The marketing mix traditionally comprised the '4Ps': Product, Price, Place and Promotion. Today, it is considered that there are a wider range of issues to address. Together, these 'six Ps' form the structure for your marketing programme:

**Product:** The package of benefits that you are offering customers. Step 5 is about planning your online content and services. Step 8 is about your brand, and choice of domain name. Step 10 looks at web site design.

**Price:** A tough choice as internet companies have regrouped and repositioned following the dot.com crisis of 2000. The marketing objectives you chose in Steps 2 and 4 will inform your choice. Step 5 discusses ecommerce and pricing.

**Place:** Concerns your domain name, covered in Step 8; and making sure you can be found through search engines, covered in Step 12; together with setting up effective fulfilment systems (whether online, for serving content, or physical, for delivering goods). There are also issues about compliance with legal requirements in other countries where users might access your web site, dealt with in Step 11.

**Promotion:** Communication with customers and other stakeholders. Step 12 covers online and offline promotion in depth.

**People:** Your staff and business partners play a key role in ensuring the success of your web site. Step 6 explains how you can ensure buy-in. Step 7 offers a guide to choosing and using consultants.

**Processes:** Perceptions of your web site - and of your business - will be determined by how well the technology works, and Step 9 discusses the choices. Logistics and customer service to support the web site are also key factors, touched on in Step 5.

## Marketing resources

There is a profusion of resources available if you want to understand marketing theory and practice in more depth, or if you simply want to keep up to date:

- The Chartered Institute of Marketing at www.cim.co.uk has an authoritative range of publications and training seminars; can suggest consultants to help you and offers professional marketing qualifications.

- Online marketing resources include *Adweek* magazine's www.technology marketing.com; the US-based Internet Marketing Centre's www.marketing tips.com; *Marketing Magazine*'s online marketing information at www. marketing.haynet.com; review sites such as www.clickz.com; *Internet*

*Magazine*'s web marketing news at www.internet-sales.com/hot; as well as sites of other magazines, such as www.mediaweek.com.

- Books exist on all aspects of marketing, so browse the CIM site or bookshop and library shelves to find one that most suits you.

- Take advantage of the services available to all businesses from the local Chamber of Commerce or Business Link (see www.businesslink.co.uk for details). Low cost training, free advice and consultancy packages are available in many areas.

# Internet: the basics

## Where to start

Familiarity with the internet environment is essential if you are to make the most of this medium. The range of resources to help you is very wide, and includes:

- The BBC's www.bbc.co.uk/webwise, which includes business advice, links and case studies.

- Online tutorials and guides offered by internet and IT corporations, including www.microsoft.com and www.netscape.com.

- Specialist sites providing free online training and information, for example, in HTML, basic web design, graphics etc. The best include Webmonkey at http://hotwired.lycos.com/webmonkey/; explanations of internet and IT jargon at www.webopaedia.com or www.whatis.com; About.com at http://webdesign.about.com/compute/webdesign, or www.learnthat.com/courses/computer/developer.shtml.

- Government sponsored sites www.businessadviceonline.org and www.ukonlineforbusiness.gov.uk, which have a wealth of factsheets and case studies.

- Technical resources for web development and free software are widely available on the internet, at sites such as:

  http://hotwired.lycos.com/webmonkey

www.freewarefiles.com

www.download.com

www.netmag.co.uk lists others

Keep up to date with publications like 'Internet Magazine'

- You can create simple web sites free of charge using sites such as www.bigfoot.com, www.homestead.com and www.geocities.com, who provide a 'wizard' to create your web site, which they then host for you.

- Low cost training, free advice and fixed price consultancy packages, provided by your local:

    - college or university;
    - small business advisory service or Business Link (see www.businesslink.co.uk for details);

       - Chamber of Commerce;

       - library.

- Books such as *The Rough Guide to the Internet* (which has some free content at www.roughguides.com/Internet).

## Keeping up to date

Print resources to help you keep up to date include monthlies like *Internet Magazine* at www.internet-magazine.com; weeklies like *New Media Age* at www. nma.co.uk or *IT Week* at www.zdnet.co.uk/itweek. There are also weekly online supplements carried by most of the broadsheet newspapers. Many have supporting web sites with free content.

Free online internet news services include www.theregister.co.uk and www.netimperative.com (the *Industry Standard* at www.thestandard.com closed in summer 2001). Simply visit their sites and register your details.

## Statistics, surveys, reports

Statistics and research on the internet industry, and on users, are published by many companies, including the following:

- www.forrester.com

- www.Internetindicators.com

- www.jupiterMMXI.com

- www.nielsen-netratings.com

- www.nua.net/surveys

- www.pewInternet.org

You can buy full reports from these sites, but they all publish free summaries, highlights and key statistics.

A major government survey of 9,000 companies and their ecommerce activity was published in May 2001 at www.statistics.gov.uk.

## Which are the best internet sites?

You can see what is rated as cool on the internet at the following sites:

- www.roughguides.com/Internet (see the Directory)
- http://home.netscape.com/netcenter/cool
- www.guardianunlimited.co.uk/index/webguides
- www.coolsiteoftheday.com
- www.thenetnow.co.uk
- www.netmag.co.uk (see 'Sites' for their listings)
- www.killersites.com
- www.top10links.com
- www.web100.com
- www.toptensites.com

Competition and award winning sites enable you to learn from market leaders. Some are listed in the section on Competitions in Step 12 - Promotion.

Two excellent books, readable, packed with design ideas and backed by technical information, are:

*Designing Web Usability* by Jakob Nielsen - New Riders

*Creating Killer Web Sites* by David Siegal - Hayden Books

Design ideas and guidance are offered by sites such as:

- www.useit.com (Jakob Neilsen's site)
- www.mediainspiration.com

- www.projectcool.com

- www.webpagesthatsuck.com

Monthlies like *Internet Magazine* and internet columns in many newspapers and magazines review sites and offer listings.

Books such as *The Internet Atlas* (which lists a thousand web sites, with colour screenshots) and other directories are useful sources.

There are many 'best of the web' sites to help you benchmark

# What is the future for marketing online?

Markets are now mature and global and as a result, customers are more sophisticated. In future, the most powerful brands will be customer-centric. Successful companies will know the customer and will be the customer's advocate.

Competitive advantage will come from understanding customers and the market - not from products or from service.

The internet has given the customer speed, choice, control and comparability. It is changing the way businesses and the public buy and use products and services. But what is its commercial future?

- Tony Blair's target is that all government services will be provided online by 2005. But few taxpayers have so far used the facility to submit their tax returns online.

- The year 2000 saw a trail of dot.com failures, and blame and recrimination as investors saw share values collapse. Casualties included *The Industry Standard*, the magazine that epitomised the internet boom, which closed down in August 2001.

- Low cost airline EasyJet sells 80 per cent of its seats online, while publishers Reed Elsevier expect that within two or three years, 60 per cent of its legal publishing revenue, and 85 per cent in the case of science, will come from its online services.

- UK companies are sceptical about the value of the internet as a business tool, and in 2000, the UK's ecommerce activity totalled only half a per cent of total sales (excluding financial services). Business-to-business online exchanges have not, after all, come to dominate the procurement market.

- But experts continue to predict that the internet will soon shift to a new paradigm where it will be accepted that users pay for online content. Improvements in technology, such as mobile internet access, and use of broadband, are also expected to play a part in reviving the market.

The current uncertainty in the internet economy simply underlines the need to address in a methodical way the issues about your markets, goals and audiences.

# Part 2

Strategy and Planning

# Part 2

## Strategy and Planning

## Step 1: Where are you now? Auditing your position

### Summary

- How to do a formal marketing audit
- Market research
- Benchmarking and statistics online

First, you'll need to work out where you are currently positioned in relation to your customers and the marketplace, your marketing activity (online and offline) and the internet. Once you understand where you are now, Steps 2 and 3 will help you decide where you want to be.

## Marketing and your business

### Carry out a formal review

Undertaking a review is vital as it will ensure a methodical approach. Firstly, it gathers all the information you need to determine how your business can succeed in its markets and secondly, it evaluates your position, using a 'SWOT' (strengths, weaknesses, opportunities and threats) analysis, for example. As a result, you will be able to make objective evidence-based choices about how you will spend your limited marketing resources to best effect.

Establishing a project team makes sense even at this early stage, as discussed in Step 6 about people.

# A marketing audit

Begin by carrying out a marketing audit, which should cover:

**The market:** Its size, whether it is growing and at what speed, customers' needs etc. What is the state of the online market for your products and services? Do you know your customers' attitudes to the internet, whether they have internet access, how they would use suppliers' sites, their willingness to buy online?

**Competition:** Who your major competitors are, their current offerings and future plans, market share, what differentiates their service from yours, their marketing activity. What business are they doing online? How does their internet site compare to your own?

**Environment:** Background factors, economic and financial, legal and regulatory, social and technological. How familiar are you with the internet environment?

**Your own business:** Your products and services, market share, views of your customers, resources available. How is your 'brand' perceived? What marketing activity have you carried out in the past, with what results? If you already have an online presence, do you have traffic statistics; have you obtained new customers as a result and how has the site been promoted to date?

The next section, about your business and the internet, will help you analyse your internet positioning in more depth.

# Market research

If your marketing audit reveals gaps in your information, market research can help you establish:

- What people say about your firm - what are your strengths and weaknesses?

- Who are your competitors - and what are their strengths and weaknesses?

Market research need not be expensive or elaborate. Possibilities include:

- One-to-one meetings with key customers.

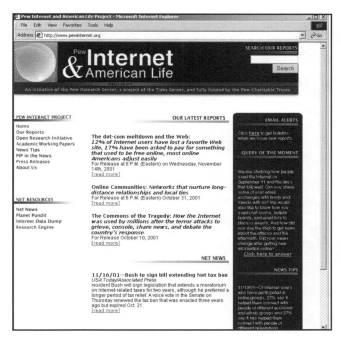

Research and data will help you understand the net and the audience

- Telephone or postal questionnaires.

- Focus group meetings with a representative sample of customers or potential customers (conducted by an independent professional researcher - these can cost around £500 per session).

- Inclusion of questions in national omnibus surveys, conducted by research organisations such as BMRB, Gallup, ICM, MORI or NOP (typically, these cost from £800 per question).

- Purchasing off-the-shelf market sector surveys from companies such as Mintel.

## SWOT analysis

Next, carry out a SWOT analysis using the data from the marketing audit. This will tell you how you can take advantage of future changes in the marketplace, and what you can do to avoid competitive disadvantage. There are three stages:

1. List the strengths, weaknesses, opportunities and threats for each of the key factors in the marketing audit.

2. Consider what the implications are for each of them: what does each mean for your business?

3. Decide what actions are needed, on the basis of what each means for your business.

## Benchmarking online

What are competing businesses doing online? Reviewing competitors' sites is an essential part of your market audit. Find them through:

- online directories, such as www.yell.com;

- carrying out internet searches for the type of product or service you provide;

- trade directories and trade association membership listings.

If you want to benchmark your own internet site, go to Step 14 for a checklist.

## Audit the internet!

E-commerce has yet to take off, according to a major government survey of 9,000 companies and their ecommerce activity (more details are given in Step 5). Your formal review will therefore need to evaluate the condition of the internet environment, especially in your own business sector.

Statistics and research on the internet industry, and on users, are published by many companies. These firms are listed on page 11 for your information.

More data on who uses the internet is given in Step 3 on defining your audience. But first you need to define your goals for your internet site: where do you want to be?

# Step 2: Where do you want to be? Defining your goals

## Summary

- First, revisit your overall business goals
- Next, you can decide your goals for the internet
- Think about your 'brand' and replicating it online
- Match your website to your overall marketing goals

## What do you want your web site to do for you...and for your customers?

Is your site marketing you, or are you marketing it? How will the web site relate to your overall marketing strategy? What do you want it to achieve for your business? How do you expect it to benefit your customers? A clear and agreed purpose for your web site is essential, and Step 2 will help you define it.

If you expect large numbers of new customers to materialise effortlessly, you are likely to be disappointed. The businesses that have done best online are those with an imaginative and customer focused approach. But a web site will help you pre-empt the threats of invisibility or competitive disadvantage you'll face as more and more people use the internet to choose products and services.

## What overall goals does your business have?

Your web site's purpose and your marketing activity should support the purposes of your business. The ability to answer the following questions will demonstrate that you are confident about your overall direction - and at a simple, practical level, the answers will enable you to brief web designers, PR consultants and others:

1. **Strengths and competitive advantage:** What is different or unique about what you do or how you do it?

2. **Customers:** Is your objective to expand your customer base, and if so, who are

you targeting? Alternatively, do you intend to increase the business that you do with existing customers?

3. **Products and services:** Which lines will you develop and which are less important? Are new innovations planned?

4. **Market:** In which market or location do you compete? Do you want to enter new markets or expand geographical reach? Are you expecting to grow sales or market share?

5. **Profitability:** What are your financial objectives? What are your shareholders' expectations?

6. **Resources:** Will you need to acquire capital, physical space or equipment? Do new processes or technologies need to be developed?

7. **People:** Do you plan to increase management and staffing complement, skills, performance or productivity?

8. **Values and beliefs:** Do you have ethical standards, a culture or style of management that underpins all your activities?

9. **Public image:** How do you want to be perceived by staff, the community and competitors?

## Your business goals for the internet

These are some of the opportunities that the internet offers your firm:

**Secure your business's future:**

- Punch above your weight; many small firms have better sites than large ones.

- Avoid competitive disadvantage, ensuring you're not missed off customers' shortlists simply because you're invisible online.

- Develop a cool modern image, differentiating yourself from more traditional images.

**Provide new and different services, attracting new customers:**

- Widen the reach of a specialist product way beyond your own locality.

- Provide new types of interactive service.

- Sell documents or information online.

**Improve communication:**

- Reach new and existing clients more cost-effectively.

- Be available 24 hours a day, seven days a week.

- Build customer loyalty: keep customer relationships alive with updates on your products and services or the market.

- Increase customer confidence by providing order status reports online and by publishing details of prices, stock levels etc.

**Become more efficient:**

- Cut the time you spend taking details of new jobs and orders by allowing customers to provide information about new matters online.

- Save your time by publishing standard information so you don't need to repeat it to every customer.

- Automate giving quotations to customers.

- Save money on printed brochures and catalogues, and take advantage of the possibility of instantaneous updating offered by the web.

- Cut out intermediaries and the profit margin they take by trading direct with consumers.

- Use emails, with links back to your web site, to avoid the costs of fulfilling printed direct mail.

- Gain valuable statistics and feedback on your services.

- Help staff recruitment.

## Positioning your business: your brand

People have an image of your business, even if yours is not a household name. That image will influence them and their decision whether or not to use you or recommend you, and it will govern their expectations of you. Step 1 may have helped you get to know the images people have of you, so you can now decide what, if anything, you want to change about your image. How would you like customers to describe your business?

From the customer's perspective, a brand provides an image that matches their aspirations. It guides the selection of a product or service and offers assurance and quality. It also enables them to project values with which they can identify and offers membership of a 'club'.

Brands are valuable, in total worth around 25 per cent of the world's wealth. When Ford bought Jaguar, it was estimated that only 16 per cent of the purchase cost was represented by physical assets.

Online customers rate brands as less important than the population as a whole, according to Total Research Inc. They like innovative, exciting, intelligent, international brands.

Four issues are the key to your brand. These will help you determine how you would like your brand to be perceived. You will have found the answers in Step 1.

## 1. Core qualities

- What do you promise in relation to your products or services? What benefits do they offer to customers?

- How do you compare to competitors?

- Why should customers select you or your products rather than others?

These factors require choices and consensus in the business about its products and services, and how these are presented. These choices need to be based on evidence about the market.

## 2. Tangible, visible branding

- Your business name and domain name (see Step 8).

- Statements about your values and standards.

- What the web site itself looks and feels like (see Step 10).

- Your logo, if you have one.

- The appearance of your letterhead and other print material.

- PR and advertising.

- Packaging.

- Your premises, vehicles etc.

- How distinctive, relevant, memorable and flexible are these?

Relatively easy to change, these can remain superficial and are vulnerable to being undermined by failure to live up to the standards they promote, and to inconsistent use within your business.

## 3. Performance

- What actual product or service quality is experienced by the customer?

- How do they perceive cost and value?

- Customer service.

- How does performance compare to the promises made for the products or services, and the values that the firm says it has?

Although intangible and hard to measure, these have the greatest influence on perceptions of the firm.

## 4. Consistency and coherence

- Is your brand presented in a cohesive way?

- Do you apply your brand consistently across all channels?

- Is your online brand consistent with your existing brand positioning?

- Alternatively, is there a case for an entirely new online brand, as discussed in Step 8, in relation to domain names?

- If you alter your brand, do you pay attention to what already exists?

- Do you ensure that your brand is respected internally as well as used externally?

The less methodical you are in applying your brand consistently, the less recognition you will gain from it and the less value it will add to your business.

This law firm has chosen a brand image that's very different from the traditional solicitors'

## Your marketing goals for your web site

You probably expect that your site will help get your firm noticed and bring you new clients. But with internet sites closing daily, and search engines struggling to provide order in the impenetrable online jungle, the marketing relationship between your firm and your web site is much more complex. Consider what you're trying to achieve:

1. Support a 'call to action'? Your conventional advertising and PR can promote the web site as an easy way for potential clients to contact your firm to find

out more about their rights or risks.

2. Cement client relationships? Follow up letters, emails or newsletters to clients can encourage customers to visit the site to check up on new legal developments, for example, encouraging client loyalty and 'word of mouth' referrals.

3. Unique selling point? Marketing can emphasise the value that your web site will add to the service clients will receive; the online matter status report is an example of a unique selling point that might persuade someone to choose one firm, rather than another.

4. Substantive service offered? Does your site offer a stand-alone service (model documents, DIY claims packs etc.) which will deserve marketing support in its own right.

Having determined your goals for your web site, you can now focus on the users.

# Step 3: Who is your audience? Market segmentation

## Summary

- Choose a target audience on which to focus your website
- Your customers are one audience - there are others too
- B2B, B2C, C2B and P2P: online business models explained
- Get to know the online population and what they are like
- The 'product life-cycle': where are your customers on the technology curve?

## You can't be all things to all people

Design your web site around the users and what they'll find useful. Don't design it around your own view of your products and services, or the way your business is organised.

Picture imaginary users and how your site might address their worries or fit in with their lifestyle. Approach real people to ask what they would like.

To meet the needs of users effectively, you will have to choose which users you want to target. Your site can't be all things to all people. For example:

- Will you concentrate on serving existing customers or enticing new ones?

- What socio-economic groups have you in mind? Age? Race and religion? Lifestyle (hedonist, liberal educated etc.)? Family responsibilities (single, young married, family with young children, empty nesters, sole survivors)? Financial position? Benefits sought?

- For business-to-business services, what size of business, industrial/commercial sector, ownership status?

- How IT literate do you expect visitors to be?

- Is the focus to be on business people or private individuals?

- What about people other than customers?

Get to know the demographics of internet users (discussed below) to help you choose the best way to target your site.

## Targeting visitors who aren't customers

The internet is also a cost-effective channel for developing relationships with a range of groups. Professor Adrian Payne proposes a 'six markets model':

- **Customers:** existing and potential, who will remain the prime focus for marketing activity.

- **Referral sources:** 'The best marketing is that which is carried out by your own customers; that is why the customer loyalty ladder is so important'. Online, 'viral marketing' has encouraged word-of-mouth promotion by customers. You may have many other referral sources and the web enables their sites to be linked to yours.

- **Suppliers:** You can use your web site to help your procurement by providing information for suppliers and offering new ways in which you can collaborate with them.

- **Recruitment:** Skills shortages remain, while unsolicited CVs and job applications can be an administrative burden. Your web site can be designed to help you reach and attract the right people.

- **Opinion-formers:** Your image with shareholders, venture capitalists, finance analysts or regulators may be important. Any business can develop its web site as a source of authoritative information and comment for use by journalists. Remember that local newspapers sell more copies in their area than *The Sun*!

- **The internal market:** Integration of your web site with your business, and its successful promotion, will be helped by staff awareness. Also, staff are usually internal customers themselves.

## B2B, B2C, C2B or P2P?

There are four basic models for ecommerce and are defined by the parties involved:

- **B2B** - Business-to-business: Supplying products and services to other businesses. According to the ecommerce surveys quoted in Step 1, this is the predominant model in the UK.

- **B2C** - Business-to-consumer: Retailing online direct to private consumers. Examples are Amazon.com (books etc.), Dell (computers) and Charles Schwab (share dealing). This sector has suffered the greatest impact from the dot.com crisis. The surveys mentioned in Step 1 show that the greatest volume of B2C activity is in financial services.

- **C2B** - Consumer-to-business: Reversing the usual customer/supplier relationship. At Priceline, for example, would-be travellers name the price they are prepared to pay for flights and hotels, and suppliers decide whether to accept.

- **P2P** - Peer-to-peer, or consumer-to-consumer: The web site acts as an intermediary, enabling individuals to trade between themselves. Examples are auction sites like eBay.com and the MP3 music exchanges such as Napster.

## Who are your online visitors, and what are they like?

Take account of how your internet audience will differ from your traditional clientele. To do this:

- Make use of the wealth of data about use of the internet, from the sources highlighted in Step 1.

- Review statistics from your own web site, if you have one, as described in Step 14.

- Obtain feedback from visitors to your site, as proposed in Step 14.

Remember that the online audience is global, affluent, impatient, intolerant, demanding, fickle, self-interested and over-informed.

### Who uses the internet?

The internet survey agency www.mmxi.com reported in March 2001 that:

- 11 million people in the UK use the web now, a 40 per cent increase in the year up to September 2000.

- 6 hours 48 minutes are spent online every month by the average user - a 35 per cent increase over the last year.

- 32 per cent of households shop online.

- The fastest growing user group are the 2 to 14 year olds.

- Women are catching up with men online: 49 per cent of users are men over 15 years of age; 36 per cent are women over 15; and 15 per cent are 2 to 14 year olds.

Households headed by a professional are more than twice as likely to have used the web as those headed by an unskilled worker, the Office for National Statistics www.statistics.gov.uk reported in January 2001.

## 'Silver surfers'

In March 2001, the Barclays Consumer Internet Confidence Survey (compiled with NOP) found that the confidence of internet users aged over 55 is increasing, while amongst other age groups it is dropping. Men aged 55 or over typically spend half an hour more online per month than other age groups.

## The internet at work

3 million people in the UK access the web from work (says Jupiter MMXI). In the US, 162 million people accessed the internet at home, compared to 41 million at work (according to Neilson/NetRatings).

According to the April 2001 issue of a new magazine for self-employed people www.alodis.com, technology is a key enabler for this group, and therefore an important channel for reaching them. Here are some statistics:

- 85 per cent of self-employed people use a computer for business, compared to the average of 24 per cent who do so.

- 75 per cent of self-employed people use the internet and email for work, compared to only 16 per cent of the general public.

- However, only 25 per cent of the self-employed have their own web site.

E-commerce has yet to take off, according to a major government survey of 9,000 companies and their ecommerce activity (more details are given in Step 5). Your formal review will therefore need to evaluate the condition of the internet environment, especially in your own business sector.

## The product life-cycle

The 'product life-cycle' analysis can be applied both to:

- Your substantive product or service. Is it unique or innovative? Does it have wide appeal, or is it only for pioneers who like to be at the leading edge?

- Your audience's confidence on the internet. Are they tech-savvy experienced users, or are they newbies, relatively unfamiliar with the environment?

Your positioning in the 'product life-cycle' will affect how you develop your web site and promote your products and services online, and who you choose as your target audience.

Market theorists explain that new products start, develop and become commodities, their prices and market share rising and falling as they go through the cycle. Their analysis is easiest to understand in relation to new technologies, such as mobile phones; only a few years ago, these were high price items for yuppy business people; now they are low cost commodity items that even children have.

Where is your product or service in this continuum? Determining its position will help you understand the state of your market, and plan your marketing. There are four key phases:

1. **Leading edge, or innovative products or services**, which can be promoted on the basis of their uniqueness, but which will not yet have mass appeal.

2. **Product differentiation**: Competitors are appearing, but the products themselves are still different to one another, and so can be promoted on the basis of their qualities.

3. **Service differentiation**: The market is maturing, the product/service has become more standard and more popular, so differentiation is now based on customer service or branding, rather than anything intrinsic to the product/service itself.

4. **Commodity**: This is now a mass market. There is now little difference between competing products or services, so differentiation is simply on price and speed of delivery.

In this chart, each column shows a new phase in the life-cycle of a market or product:

| Time | First phase | Second phase | Third phase | Fourth phase |
|---|---|---|---|---|
| Market share | Innovators 2.5 per cent | Early adopters 13.5 per cent | Early majority 34 per cent | Late majority 34 per cent |
| Characteristic | Unique | Product differentiation | Service differentiation | Commodity |
| Marketing focus | Explain the new product | Compete with others | Brand values | Corporate |
| Sales | Pioneering | Relative benefits | Relationship based | Availability based |
| Distribution | Direct selling | Exclusive distribution | Mass distribution | 80:20 |
| Price | Very high | High | Medium | Low |
| Competition | None | Few | Many | Fewer, bigger, global |
| Costs | Very high | Medium | Medium/low | Very low |
| Profit | Medium/high | High | High/medium | Medium/low |
| Management style | Visionary | Strategic | Operational | Cost management |

Source: Professor Malcolm McDonald, Cranfield School of Management, based on Wilson M, Marketing Improvements Group.

## Do your market research

Test your ideas, however informally, with your target audience. What will visitors want from you? Will people find your site useful, will they visit and will they give you business as a result?

# Step 4: How do you get where you want to be? Writing your marketing objectives

## Summary

- Define your objectives clearly at the outset
- You can then choose marketing activity, and evaluate success

Now, having completed Steps 1, 2 and 3, you are in a position to spell out exactly *what* is to be accomplished by your marketing activities. Step 5 onwards will enable you to determine *how* those marketing objectives can be achieved.

Without planned and documented objectives it will be impossible to make informed and cost-effective choices, and it will be impossible to know whether you have achieved what you set out to do. As with a journey without a defined destination, any direction is as good as any other, and you'll be unable to tell whether you've arrived.

Documenting your marketing objectives will ensure three things:

1.  Marketing activities can all be related to an overall purpose, ensuring effective focus.

2.  Everyone involved will be able to direct their efforts to common ends, which are known and defined.

3.  Later, you will be able to measure results, judge value for money and evaluate success.

Objectives should be 'SMART', as follows:

- **Specific:** Goals to be achieved should be clear and identifiable.

- **Measurable:** There should be a quantifiable way to determine whether the objective has been achieved.

- **Achievable:** Objectives should be realistic, even if challenging.

- **Relevant:** They should relate to the overall goals of your business and relate directly to your markets, customers, products and services.

- **Timed:** Dates for completion and for significant milestones should be specified.

## Sample objectives

In Step 2, we looked in outline at online marketing objectives. Some specific examples could include the following:

- Increase the number of unique visitors to the web site by 40 per cent within the next 12 months.

- Encourage at least 1,000 visitors to register for the email newsletter by 1 September.

- Ensure that at least 75 per cent of customers on our database have visited our site within two months following the relaunch.

- Generate 10 per cent of our sales from the web site by the year end.

- Double the number of customer orders from outside the M25 area within six months.

- Establish the perception that our web site is user-friendly and provides information that is helpful in its own right.

- At least half the agencies in the sector should know that orders can be placed through our web site by Christmas.

## Your marketing plan

The next step is to match these objectives to the right marketing mix, explained in the remaining steps. Documenting your intended activities for Steps 5-14, together with your objectives, will complete your marketing plan.

# Part 3

## Your Marketing Mix

# Part 3

## Your Marketing Mix

## Step 5:  Planning your content and services

### Summary

- Step 5 addresses the 'Product' issue in the '4Ps' approach to marketing

- Key choices to be made at this stage are about:

  - Price - another of the '4Ps' - and how much content should be free of charge on your web site, and whether you attempt to sell information, products or services online

  - Relationships - how far you will take advantage of the web's interactivity to build relationships with customers

- The six web site models from which you can choose are:

  a.  Brochure
  b.  Information-rich
  c.  Interactive
  d.  Ecommerce
  e.  The virtual business
  f.  Extranets

- Customers can be given the confidence to buy online from you, if you adopt the right approach

## Content is king

Think about your own use of the internet and you'll acknowledge that the sites you visit most are those offering substantive content: information, updates, services and interaction. Content is king.

## Pricing for the internet

In the wake of the dot.com crisis in 2000, decisions about pricing online are tough:

- Should online content (information, updates, downloads, reports) be offered free of charge?

- Should you differentiate prices for your products and services purchased online, from prices on orders received through conventional channels?

Here are some of the factors you must bear in mind:

- **Branding:** Pricing is not just about recovering costs or generating profit. Pricing plays an important role in the image of your service and people's perceptions of quality and value. Are your products or services 'reassuringly expensive' or 'never beaten on price'?

- **Internet culture:** Internet culture currently assumes free content. Providers continue to believe that the market is not yet ready to pay for content, unless it is highly specialised. Pearson, for example, has set itself firmly against charging for the basic services offered by www.FT.com - even though reports in April 2001 suggested that the FT.com site had cost £155m and generated only £18m in revenue. But increasingly, commentators believe that providers will soon begin to require payment for mainstream services. One web site tracking the introduction of charges for content is www.TheEndOfFree.com.

- **Cannibalisation:** You may already be generating revenue from sales of printed information, consultancy fees etc. You will need to evaluate the financial impact on your business if you now cannibalise that revenue, and publish material online that is free or low cost.

- **Revenue from advertising:** Before the dot.com crisis, online business models assumed that free content and services would attract large audiences. At that time, you could charge premium rates to advertisers keen to reach those audiences, generating profit. However, the effectiveness of online advertising is increasingly in question. Groups like Yahoo and Excite@Home have seen shrinking advertising revenues, to the extent that the latter filed for bankruptcy in September 2001.

- **Increasing your audience:** Use your site to publish information not just on your products and services but also on related issues and you will attract a wider audience. Positioning yourself as a helpful one stop information point will enhance your image.

- **Channel conflict:** If you are selling products or services through traditional channels, as well as online, there can be conflicts in the way that online and offline pricing and service relate to one another.

- If you use **retailers or agents**, or employ sales people, what impact will they expect direct internet sales to have on their own position? Can you present your ecommerce plans to them in a positive way?

- Expectations are that internet prices are lower, and **comparison shopping** (finding the lowest price and best features) is made easy online. If you differentiate online and offline prices, the rationale will need to be clear to customers and staff.

- **Extra costs for fulfilment etc:** If you have your own retail outlet, or sell through wholesalers, have you fully costed the arrangements for fulfilling individual online orders? Personal shoppers carry their goods home at no cost to you; online orders will need to take account of home delivery costs.

## Ecommerce has yet to take off

Should you invest in ecommerce functionality on your site? Ecommerce systems can cost much less than you would expect, but bear in mind that, according to a major government survey of 9,000 companies, ecommerce has yet to take off in the UK.

Findings of the government's survey, published in May 2001 at www.statistics.gov.uk include the following:

- 92 per cent of respondents use PCs etc.

- 63 per cent have web access.

- 61 per cent have a web site.

- 33 per cent make ecommerce purchases.

- 16 per cent make ecommerce sales; 66 per cent of the remainder do not plan to do so in the next year.

- 600 businesses carried out over half of their work activities online.

Barriers to use of the internet for business were identified by the research:

- 40 per cent of companies said the cost was too high.

- 38 per cent could not see any benefit.

- 32 per cent were concerned about staff misuse.

- 27 per cent thought that the web was too slow or unstable.

- 27 per cent believed that the costs were too high.

The results also demonstrate the modest scale of the ecommerce economy:

- Internet sales were worth £56.6bn annually in the UK, of which £42.7bn is finance/insurance. That amounts to two per cent of total sales, or only 0.46 per cent of sales if you exclude finance/insurance sales

- B2C (sales to households) are worth only £10bn in total, of which £8.8bn is finance/insurance.

Europe has 19 million SMEs (small to medium enterprises, with fewer than 250 employees), making up 99 per cent of the total number of businesses. An April 2001 survey by Gallup for the EU found that:

- only 70 per cent have internet access;

- fewer than a third are involved in ecommerce.

## Relationship marketing

The internet is an ideal medium for building relationships. Since the 1980s, marketing has increasingly acknowledged the importance of 'relationship marketing' with customers, in contrast to traditional 'transactional marketing', emphasising customer acquisition and sales.

Professor Adrian Payne of Cranfield University has been one of the most articulate advocates of relationship marketing. In his book *The Essence of Services Marketing* (Prentice Hall, 1993), he explains that existing customers 'are easier to sell to and are frequently more profitable', but businesses still place more emphasis and resources on acquiring new customers, while taking existing customers for granted. He suggests that there is a 'loyalty ladder', which customers can be moved up. The rungs of the ladder are as follows:

1.  Prospect: a potential customer.

2.  Customer: a one-off purchaser.

3.  Client: repeat purchaser.

4.  Supporter: loyal purchaser.

5.  Advocate: actively promotes you to third parties.

The two approaches are contrasted by Professor Payne as follows:

| *Transaction marketing* | *Relationship marketing* |
| --- | --- |
| Focus on single sale | Focus on customer retention |
| Product features emphasised | Product benefits emphasised |
| Short term | Long term |
| Customer service not first concern | Customer service a priority |
| Limited customer commitment | High customer commitment |
| Moderate customer contact | Frequent customer contact |
| Quality is for production | Quality is the concern of all |

## Six models for business web sites

Here are six models for business web sites providing varying levels of content and service:

### a) The brochure site: who you are and what you do

This is the entry-level site, offering static information about products and services, office locations, your people etc. Even at this level, you can use the internet to make yourself more customer-friendly by including details such as:

- direct-dial and mobile numbers, and individual email addresses for your key people or departments;

- location maps and directions;

- updated price lists;

- who to contact when something goes wrong with your product or service;

- and don't forget your land and postal addresses, which are left off a surprising number of sites!

A simple brochure site is better than no site at all. Substantive content or interactive services will certainly attract more visitors, but without a site, you just will not make it onto the shortlist of any potential customer using the web to screen suppliers.

Simple web sites operated by small companies can achieve remarkable success:

www.classics-car-hire.co.uk is a two person business in Ilkley, Yorkshire that attracts 90 per cent of its business through the internet.

www.raymears.com advertises survival expert's courses and equipment, and has repaid its cost over a weekend following a feature on BBC2 television.

### (b) The content rich site: giving people stuff that helps their lives

You will attract and retain more visitors if you go beyond brochure information to cover wider topics related to your products, services and marketplace:

- Start by thinking about your customers and the need they wish to satisfy, or the problem they wish to solve. These issues will lead them to consider your product or service.

- Then, think creatively about the other related issues which will typically be concerning a customer in that situation.

- Now, you can respond with a range of supporting information that provides a holistic approach to that customer.

This approach should bring the following benefits:

- Position you as a one stop shop for customers needs.

- Establish your authority in the field.

- Attract visitors, who come for free information, but who stay or return to make a purchase.

- Build customer loyalty.

This engineering company's portal does much more than just sell its products

## Focus on the customer

Some examples of sites that focus on the customer, not the product or service, are:

**www.divorce.co.uk:** Solicitors Mills & Reeve not only explain the legal process but also include information on the personal emotional side, the impact of divorce on children etc.

**www.milpro.com** sells metalworking fluids and other industrial fluids, bonded abrasive products (grinding wheels etc.), cutting tools, tool holders and related components, but the site also provides information for small workshop businesses on buying and selling used equipment, identifying new business opportunities and troubleshooting manufacturing problems.

**www.crayola.com** includes children's stories, colouring in, games etc.

**www.petcat.co.uk** is operated by Whiskas but provides comprehensive information about cats.

## What content can you publish?

Content can include:

- user-friendly guides;
- case studies;
- seminar presentations;
- press releases and articles;
- answers to frequently asked questions;
- links to other relevant resources.

## Links

Links can help your site become a first port of call if you provide links to other resources your customers are likely to need. Links provide low cost content, but be aware of the following:

- Permission is not normally required from the site to which you are linking, but avoid using 'frames' or 'deep links' which could infringe the rights of the other site's owner; see Step 11 on Risk Management for more information.

- It is normal to publish on your web site a general statement to the effect that the sites to which you are linking are not operated by you and that you are not responsible for their content.

- You should consider negotiating a reciprocal link, where appropriate (see also the discussion in Step 12 on Promotion).

- Users who follow your links to other sites may not return to yours!

Some of the best examples of links collections are hobby sites, but commercial sites can also include useful association. Please take a look at the following:

www.kfs.org/kites has lots of links to do with kite flying.

www.teddybear.com is about…well, you can guess.

www.gamesbiz.net from solicitors Osborne Clarke has links helping people in the electronic entertainment industry.

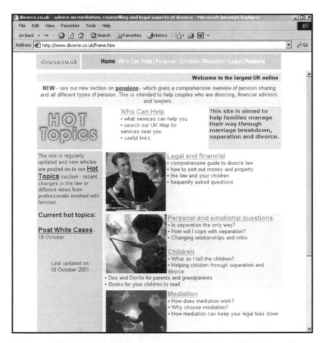

Solicitors Mills & Reeve offer a magazine style website talking about all aspects of divorce - not just the legal side

## (c) The interactive business

Interaction allows you to start a relationship with visitors to your site. Margaret Manning of internet developer www.readingroom.net says:

> Successful sites tend to be those which: understand what users want from their site; provide specific interactive areas that target those needs; and thereby hold user attention for longer, and encourage users to return. This kind of strategy is far more likely to bear fruit than the arbitrary use of flashy effects to dazzle your visitors.

Attractive interactive functionality will gain your site favourable publicity, as some of the examples here will show.

### email

An email facility is essential. Here are some tips to help you make the most of the feature on your web site:

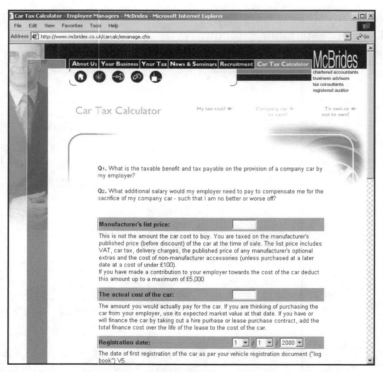

Responding to customers' wider needs can gain you publicity and visitors , as is the case with the above example from the site of McBrides,Chartered Accountants in Sidcup

- Senders regard email as an instantaneous medium and will expect a reply, or at least an acknowledgement, within a day. So have systems to ensure you are able to respond quickly. For example, arrange staff cover, email diversion or 'out of office' automated replies, so that customers' messages don't pile up in an inbox when people are absent from the office.

- Use named contacts such as abida@ rather than anonymous addresses such as sales@, because these sound more personal.

- Include email addresses or forms on individual pages throughout the site, as well as at the home page. This will encourage the customer to contact you.

You'll find much more information about using email for marketing in Step 12, on promotion activity.

## Feedback or comments box

Another essential is an email facility or webform that will prompt visitors to give you feedback about the site or about the products or services you offer. Some responses will be simple enquiries that can be turned into sales leads, or helpful suggestions for additions to the site.

Complaints about the site (for example, difficulties in finding relevant information) will be made, and the impersonal and immediate character of email communication may lead your correspondent to adopt an angry or frustrated tone! However, complaints are invaluable in helping you improve the site to meet customers' needs more effectively.

As with email, ensure that correspondents receive prompt and courteous replies.

## Online quotes or calculators

Enable customers to log details of their requirements with a system to provide an automated quote, calculation or email response. Examples include:

The redundancy pay calculator offered free by solicitors Sinclair Smith & Abson at www.saslawyers.co.uk.

A company car income tax calculator at Chartered Accountants www.mcbrides.co.uk/carcalc/emanage.cfm. The feature took just a few days to develop, but having attracted a mention in *The Times*, it gains 25,000 hits per month.

### Online ordering

Provide an order form that customers can complete online, even if payment has to be made separately (by posting a cheque, awaiting an invoice or telephoning with credit card details).

One in four UK businesses already provide this facility, according to the DTI's International Benchmarking Study 2000 (at www.ukonlineforbusiness.gov.uk).

### Decision-tree

Decision-trees, offering a series of yes/no questions, help users diagnose problems and reach information directly relevant to their situation. Examples include

www.mysimon.com, offering a sophisticated product feature and price comparison system.

www.taste.co.uk/recipe/index.jsp offers a recipe assistant.

### Visitor registration

Visitor registration can be irritating for users, unless the process is simple, and you have something of substance to offer. Updates by email, access to reports (e.g. market research), or to detailed texts, could be provided in this way.

If your online visitors can register on your web site, you must ensure that your internet service provider has a simple way to provide registration information to you, so that it can be integrated with your in-house database, and used in the same way.

A couple of solicitors' practices providing free updates, comment and information on ecommerce law and practice - subject to registration - are:

www.out-law.com, provided by Masons

www.eversheds80.com, provided by Eversheds.

This car dealer enables visitors to talk to each other and the company's engineers online

## Community

The internet thrives on information exchange and community. Enable visitors to exchange information with one another, through your site.

- Chatrooms are offered by mainstream sites, such as www.beme.com and www.confetti.com, to attract regular visitors, by making them feel involved.

- At www.mansfieldmotors.co.uk, a Land Rover dealer provides a chatroom enabling customers to buy and sell spares amongst themselves, plus a bulletin board where the firm's engineers answer technical questions.

- www.timberweb.co.uk features over 1,000 timber trade links, a company database, news etc. It has over 1,000 subscribers and the company's main revenue no longer comes from actual timber trading but from membership fees, advertising and brokerage fees generated by the web site.

Bulletin Board software (e.g. Ultimate Bulletin Board) can be purchased or some web sites (eg www.ezboard.com) offer free facilities.

Be aware that bulletin boards and chatrooms need monitoring to avoid the risk of liability for inappropriate comment posted by visitors. You will need to consider this risk, and the resources needed to counteract it. For example, how much time will be absorbed if you require all postings to be submitted to you for vetting before posting?

### Order status information

Tracking services, originated by US parcels services like UPS and Federal Express, and adopted by others such as Dell, enable customers (with a password) to use company web sites to monitor the status of their orders. Lawyers are now using the same approach, as at Hammond Suddard Edge's www.legalmove.com, which offers armchair conveyancing - but the law firm that first developed online casetracking was the small five partner practice Fidler and Pepper, based in the East Midlands, with www.fidler.co.uk.

## d) The ecommerce-enabled business

### What counts as ecommerce?

Ecommerce can be defined as a trade that actually takes place over the web. A much larger number of transactions involve the web at some state (for example, one estimate in 2000 was that only 2.7 per cent of new cars were actually purchased over the web, but 40 per cent of purchases involved use of the net to obtain information on models, compare prices etc.).

The comprehensive ecommerce survey, published by the UK's Office for National Statistics in May 2001, showed that only 2 per cent of sales were carried out online in 2000.

### What will and won't sell online?

What will sell well online:

- 'Low touch' products, which people will be happy to buy without seeing or touching beforehand. Computers, CDs, books and travel tickets are the best-selling items online.

- Items that can be delivered online: computer software, travel tickets, share-dealing, pornography, technical information (publisher Reed Elsevier's August 2001 results showed a 13 per cent leap in pre-tax profits, with the expectation that within a couple of years, 85 per cent of its science publishing revenue will come from online services, and 60 per cent of legal).

- Gifts, flowers, wine etc.

- Specialist items which would otherwise be hard to obtain, such as speciality food products, collectors' items etc.

## What will sell less well online?

- 'High touch' items: clothing and groceries are often given as examples, but catalogue purchasing has worked well since Sears Roebuck launched the first in 1888; and Tesco.com is one of the great successes of the web.

- Instant gratification items - because of the delay built in by delivery logistics.

- Products for consumers who enjoy the social experience of shopping.

## Case studies

UK Online for Business (a partnership between industry and government to help British business thrive in the information-based economy), has published a series of ecommerce case studes at www.ukonlineforbusiness.gov.uk, and they include the following:

- Jack Scaife Butcher Ltd at www.jackscaife.co.uk is a local butchers producing traditional smoked and dry cured hams and bacon. Their web site cost only £1,000 to establish, but yields 50 orders a week, and annual turnover has increased from £70,000 to £700,000. The site now offers a secure online ordering service, an online order tracking service, and information on products and prices.

- DGC Distribution Ltd at www.guvnor.com is an importer and distributor of musical instruments and accessories. Faced with a market in decline, their use of ecommerce helped produce an increase of 30 per cent in annual sales. Customers can search a product database and place orders using a shopping cart system.

## *How do you give customers the confidence to buy online?*

Surveys show that many potential e-customers are lost because ecommerce systems do not give them the confidence they need to buy online. The following will help:

1. A user-friendly, easy-to-navigate system, taking account of:

   - whether your customers will be making quick impulse purchases or specifying lengthy and complex requirements;

   - their need to know where they are in the system, and to go back and forth easily without losing information they have keyed in or obtained from searches.

2. Key information about your business on the site:

   - A real address (not just an email address or a PO Box number).

   - Statutory information (as required on letterhead: VAT number, registered office, names of proprietors, registered charity number etc.).

3. Transparent pricing information, spelling out:

   - product prices;

   - VAT and other taxes;

   - discounts;

   - insurance or other administrative charges;

   - delivery costs.

4. Terms and conditions, available for customers to check before they place an order, and in a form that they can save or print.

5. A privacy policy: A statement on your site explaining:

   - who is collecting the information: your business, or some other agency?;

   - what information you collect and retain on customers;

   - the purposes for which it is used;

   - whether it is passed on to third parties and whether customers can opt out;

   - how the privacy of the information is protected and under what conditions personal information might be disclosed;

- how customers can verify, correct or update the information;

- whether your site uses 'cookies' (the software which loads hidden information on a customer's PC, which then enables the customer to be recognised when they visit the site in future) and the consequences if a customer disables them.

You can obtain more information about privacy at www.data protection.gov.uk and see also the OECD privacy statement generator at http://cs3-hq.oecd.org/scripts/pwv3/pwhome.htm.

6.  A secure area for placing orders and giving credit card details; in addition to information on your site to confirm the security arrangements you have in place. Also, always reassure customers.

7.  Security certification may be important if you are offering ecommerce services to consumers. Trust UK at www.trustuk.org.uk is a not-for-profit scheme endorsed by the government, which businesses can join either through their trade body (if it is participating) or through the Consumers' Association scheme at www.which.net/webtrader. There are also commercial alternatives such as www.clicksure.com and others.

8.  A confirmation screen setting out details of the customer's order and payment required BEFORE completion of the transaction, which they can check, correct, save or print out before they finally place an order.

9.  A confirmation screen setting out details of the customer's order and payment required AFTER completion of the transaction, which they can save or print out.

10. An email acknowledgement (which can be automated) confirming that an order has been duly received.

11. Complaints and returns:

- Email, postal address and telephone number for customers to use if things go wrong.

- Explanation of your policy on returned goods, carriage costs and refunds.

- Details of any trade body to which you belong and to which customers can complain if they remain dissatisfied.

12. Delivery: Tell customers when their goods will arrive and ensure that they are told the delivery charge (if any) before they buy.

Don't be deterred by the need for a privacy policy: the OECD site will help you write one

## Ecommerce systems

For information on ecommerce systems, please refer to 'Step 9: Marketing technology' on pages 83-85.

## e) Extranets

Extranets use normal internet technology, but instead of being available to all on the world wide web, they can be accessed only by authorised audiences. They can be used to provide privileged information and services to one or more customers.

The right service will become indispensable to a customer's employees, creating 'electronic handcuffs' which will deter customers from switching their business to a competitor.

Good examples of sites that do this are as follows:

- www.moving-picture.com uses an extranet to publish previews of advertisements still in production, for comment by the customer.

- www.newchange.com hosts all the documents for a company transaction (flotation, merger etc.) in a secure 'virtual dealroom', enabling all parties immediate access to up-to-date material. It was established by City solicitors Allen & Overy, but the technology ought to be applicable to a range of other commercial transactions, saving costs and cutting lead times.

## f) The virtual business

In virtual businesses, systems rather than people deliver the service. The set-up costs for developing the technology and the content can be substantial. Examples include:

- Electronic file swap sites such as music exchange www.mp3.com.

- Auction sites such as www.eBay.com.

- Investment services such as www.etrade.com.

- A handful of legal advice services such as www.blueflag.com or www.nextlaw.com.

# Step 6:  People

## Summary

- Ownership and involvement internally is essential
- Create a project team
- Allocate responsibility and earmark resources
- Check the internet administration specification
- Work methodically to overcome any resistance
- Market the web site internally - not just externally

## Have you got what it takes?

When it comes to IT projects, many businesses suffer from financial constraints, lack of expertise, and aversion to change and to technology. But lack of time is probably the biggest barrier as it will take you 40 to 80 hours to plan and build your site. Marshalling your resources, and gaining buy-in, are therefore key steps.

## Ownership and involvement

The internet site must be integral to your business, so everyone has got to feel ownership and involvement. Consult and inform as the site develops. Seek ideas and content from everyone in the organisation.

Involve people in order to avoid the following problems:

- **'Cannibalisation' and 'channel conflict'**: Mentioned in the discussion of ecommerce sites on page 40, these problems can arise if the internet site and online trading appear to be competing with your business's traditional sales and distribution channels. You will need to ensure that:

  - External customers perceive the new and old channels as consistent and coherent.

  - Top management accept the business case.

  - Sales staff and others supporting the traditional channels agree to any changes to their roles, and indeed see ways in which your internet site can complement their activity.

- **'Not invented here' syndrome:** Everybody in the organisation, especially those having any contact with customers, needs to be able to talk about the web site positively and with confidence. It will be hard to achieve this, if the site is developed in isolation from staff; they will see it as imposed from outside.

## Establish a project team

Establishing a project team will help ensure:

- a spread of ownership and involvement through the business;

- a source of ideas and alternatives;

- resources for developing and delivering the project;

- co-ordination for the various contributors;

- clear responsibility and accountability.

PRINCE (Projects IN Controlled Environments) is one of a number of project management methodologies. This was developed by a government agency and the manual is available from the Stationery Office. It offers a detailed process which can be applied to both large and small projects.

Project team membership, PRINCE suggests, should reflect several interests:

- The manager with ultimate responsibility for the project, who authorises expenditure, convenes and chairs project team meetings, and accounts to top management for the progress and success of the project.

- The internal (and, represented by them, external) customers whom the project is intended to benefit, who will want to ensure that the outcomes meet their needs.

- The suppliers (staff or contractors) who are responsible for designing, developing and implementing the project.

- Project assurance: someone not directly involved in the project who can keep a check on the project's progress.

## Responsibility, resources, skills

- **Named individuals** should have documented responsibility for the web site, or specific roles in relation to it.

- **Adequate resources** should be earmarked, especially for:

  - maintenance and updating on the site;

  - handling emails and comments from the site;

  - promotion activity, such as an emailed newsletter.

- **Responsibility** for the internet site may be with the IT, information management, marketing or PR functions.

- **Technical knowledge** should be unnecessary for most roles, but use the resources listed in Step 1 on page 17 to enable people to improve their skills.

- **Internet access** for your staff is essential if you wish them to contribute ideas to the site and use it as a resource in their dealings with customers. (You should introduce a policy governing staff internet use; a free sample is available from the solicitors Masons at www.out-law.com.)

- **Develop individual staff,** at whatever level, who already have a personal interest in the internet. For example, your firm's administrative and support staff can make a huge contribution and will welcome the opportunity to progress their career and vary their work.

- **Job specifications** for IT related jobs have been published by the National Training Organisation's IT training group at www.e-skillsnto.org.uk.

## Job specification for an internet administration

- **Publishing** new content on the web site, including updating the 'What's New' section and sub-editing staff contributions to adapt them for web publication.

- **General maintenance:** Review the site regularly to identify out-of-date, conflicting, or duplicated material, gaps in information, typing errors, broken links, incorrect format or house style.

- **Internal liaison:** Encourage and assist other staff to publish their documents on the site. Circulate email updates about the site internally. Provide presentations to staff about the site as necessary.

- **Enquiries:** Handle contacts received through the 'Comments on the site' facility and other telephone and written comments or enquiries about the site itself.

- **Search engines etc:** Develop and maintain inbound links (identifying and contacting other sites which we think should include a link to ours), metatags, listings in online directories and information services, and search engine registrations.

- **Internet Site Provider liaison:** Forward change requests and monitor implementation.

- **Email news:** Prepare regular email bulletins about the site and the company and distribute using our email databases for external contacts.

- **Administration:** Take minutes and maintain action lists and project plans for the project team.

- **Statistics:** Review site-use statistics to identify trends, unmet needs and new opportunities.

- **Future development:** Collate feedback and contribute ideas for future development planning for the web site.

## Overcoming internal resistance

Tactics for dealing with resistance include the following:

- **Explain:** Avoid assuming that everyone is now familiar with the internet medium, and check for understanding of basic principles. Remember that the dot.com crisis has altered people's perceptions of the web, and your business case must take a realistic view of the current environment.

- **Consult:** Include everyone in the process. You don't need to hand over responsibility for decision-making, but you do need to explain the plans and invite comment.

- **Listen properly:** Critics may be expressing real concerns that you are able to address. Or they be open to change, if you are able to ensure that the necessary training or support is provided.

- **Be open and honest:** Resistance often occurs because people suspect that information is being withheld.

- **Take account of individuals:** Make sure you understand how the development will impact on people's jobs and ways of working, and explain this to them. Ensure that their job descriptions adequately reflect what you are asking them to do.

- **Allow time for implementation and training:** People may be anxious that they will be unable to cope with the changes. Give assurances that adequate

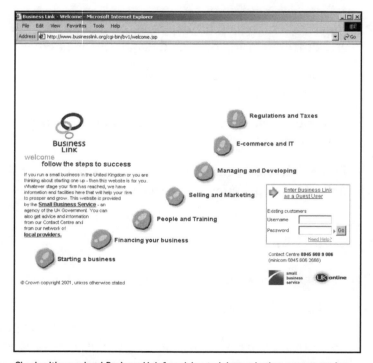

Check with your local Business Link for advice, training and other support services

training and support will be provided and that allowance will be made for reduced productivity during the transition.

- **Make the most of 'ambassadors'** in the business who can talk up the project on your behalf, and of 'quick wins' which provide visible benefits early on.

## Internal marketing

You should consider the following for internal marketing:

- A desktop icon loaded on everyone's PC with a shortcut to your site.

- Mousemats.

- An internal launch reception.

- Presentations for staff about the site and how they can benefit from it.

- Posters and flyers around the premises with screen shots.

- Internal email or memos with answers to Frequently Asked Questions (FAQs), news and updates about the site.

## External resources

- Take advantage of the services available to all businesses from the local Chamber of Commerce or Business Link (see www.businesslink.co.uk for details). Low cost training, free advice and consultancy packages are available in many areas.

- New graduates, undergraduates, even school students are worth considering: they are web savvy and eager to establish their dot.com track records, although they will require clear guidance and your supervision.

- Guidance on engaging consultants and designers is given in the next section.

# Step 7: Resources

## Summary

- Be methodical when choosing external consultants, designers or internet developers

- Agree a contract to ensure the end result is what you want

## When to use consultants/designers/internet developers

The simplicity and wide availability of internet design and publication packages allow non-specialists and amateurs to create effective web sites. Engaging external consultants to help with design, development or PR will be more costly, but can offer advantages:

- The result should be more professional.

- You will have access to expertise in web technologies and the constraints of the internet.

- It will save you time and inconvenience, and be completed more quickly.

- You will have the benefit of objective external advice.

This section provides tips on the selection process and contractual details. You can refer to Step 1 for sources of other online and offline help with both marketing and internet activity (see page 17).

## Guidelines and model documents

- The Computer Services and Software Association at www.cssa.co.uk has publications including contract guidelines.

- A number of legal web sites offer standard contractual documents for purchase and free guidance. These include www.briffa.com, www.out-law.com, www.desktoplawyer.co.uk, www.eversheds80.com, www.lawrights.co.uk and www.infolaw.co.uk, or in the US www.findlaw.com. The best place for finding solicitors to match your needs is the Law Society's www.solicitors-online.com.

## Fourteen questions to ask web designers

Margaret Manning, of internet developers www.readingroom.net, highlights the questions which will help you find a committed, business-focused web design company:

1. **Can you see their portfolio?** Do you like the other sites they have built? Are they quick to download and easy to navigate? Would your customers like them?

2. **What makes their agency different?** Do they specialise in design, a particular technology or industry sector? Which is most important to you?

3. **Are they really interested in producing your site?** Is the agency offering original ideas in their proposal, or is it a standard document?

4. **What will they expect from me?** Will you be expected to specify everything in detail, or will you get help to develop your ideas? Is there a clear timetable for you to write content, attend meetings, sign off designs etc?

5. **Can they provide the functionality your site requires?** If you need an interactive database or content management system, for example, do they have the skills to develop it?

6. **Can they advise on ecommerce systems?** Is there one particular solution they will recommend? Or will they help match your requirements to the right system?

7. **Who owns the completed site?** You may not want to stay with this web designer or internet service provider forever. If you want to move your web site, will you have rights to the content, designs and images, the code and functional components that make up the site?

8. **What are their payment terms?** Make sure you have the proposed payment terms and other terms of business in writing.

9. **What continuing costs will there be?** As well as the fees for initial development, what will be the annual charges for hosting, maintenance etc?

If your site increases in size, or if traffic increases, what are the implications for hosting costs?

10. **How long will it take?** Ensure a timetable is agreed, perhaps with a penalty clause in the event of late completion.

11. **Will it be possible to find the site on the major search engines?** As explained in Step 9 (Marketing/technology), some web site formats are more search-engine friendly than others. Can the designer advise on these choices? Ask for example sites and carry out internet searches for them, using relevant key words.

12. **Will site statistics be available?** Ask the agency to show you samples of the type of report on visits to the site that they can provide. Will these be available retrospectively or in real time? Will there be a cost for producing reports?

13. **How will you maintain the site?** To keep your site fresh, new content is required regularly. Make sure that you will not be charged prohibitively high rates for publishing updates if the agency will be doing this for you. Better still, ask about systems to enable you to maintain the site in-house, check what training or experience will be required, and whether support will be available, and at what cost.

14. **How much will it cost?** You will find that quoted costs vary remarkably. Look for value for money, not necessarily the lowest price. And as Reading Room's Margaret Manning concludes:

> Beware of the 'too good to be true' deals - that's usually just what they are!

## The selection process

Selection will involve the following steps:

1. Decide on the process and supporting documents (see above).

2. Identify designers and developers from:

   • your own favourite web sites;

   • recommendations from colleagues;

• specialist trade sites which may include listings of designers or developers who have been involved in relevant sites.

3. Meet or visit prospective suppliers.

4. Issue an Invitation to Tender document (described below).

5. Make your selection, using objective criteria settled in advance. Take account of:

   (a) views of the designer or developer's previous customers;

   (b) work accomplished for others;

   (c) capability of working to deadline and to budget;

   (d) understanding of your needs as a business, and of the internet environment - as well as technical proficiency.

## Your invitation to tender

An invitation to tender should cover the following:

• Introduction: Your current position, your goals for the site, and the expected benefits

• Project outline and proposed solutions:

   - Approach to implementation.

   - Risks inherent in the project.

   - Your priorities.

   - Assumptions you have made about resources, systems etc.

   - Timing.

   - Constraints, such as lack of staff time.

   - Who you see as being responsible for what.

• Project deliverables: Your detailed requirements.

• Planned contents.

- Functionality (e.g. database, search system, bulletin board, ecommerce, content management).

- Support (hosting, publishing, security).

- Other services required (e.g. design).

- Information required in response to invitation to tender, and the administration process for tenders.

- An appendix should give details of your current IT system, including any existing web site and the arrangements for operating it.

## The contract for developing the site

A contract for developing the site should cover:

- Project deliverables/service specification (based on the invitation to tender with modifications in the light of post-tender discussions with the selected contractor).

- Project management.

- Project plan/timescales.

- Populating the site:

  - Migration from an existing site
  - Publishing new content

- User testing and formal acceptance.

- Cost/payments.

## The contract for hosting the completed site

A contract for hosting the site should cover:

- Service levels:

- Management information to be provided.

- Server availability and maximum down-time.

- Support/helpdesk arrangements.

- Change control procedures.

- Charges and payments.

- Intellectual property rights in the system and content (you'll need to be able to transfer software used to support your site if you terminate the contract).

- Data protection.

- Warranties, indemnity.

- Termination grounds and procedures.

# Step 8: Choosing a domain name

## Summary

- Positioning your firm: how branding works
- Domain name endings and which to choose
- Tips on good domain names
- Problems with domain names and how to solve them
- Who controls domain names

## Your online brand

Your domain name represents your online identity, so choose with care.

However small your business, your brand surely deserves better recognition than this lawfirm, Hewstones, who have accorded themselves with http://easyweb.easynet .co.uk/~hewstone/. Many dial-up ISP packages now include a proper domain name, or they can be bought for as little as £10 so there is no excuse.

Brand values, and the development of internet brands, are discussed in Step 2.

## Who controls domain names?

ICANN (the Internet Corporation for Assigned Names and Numbers) took responsibility for overall domain name regulation in 1998. It was set up in 1996 by a US government initiative, taking over from the Internet Assigned Names Authority (IANA) and a US company Network Solutions, both of which also operated through agreements with the US government.

There are three main levels of domain names:

- Generic Top Level Domains (gTLDs), which include **dot.com** and **dot.net**. These names can be registered with US or international registrars and are not country-specific. You can find out about other gTLDs at the site of the regulator, the Internet Assigned Numbers Authority at www.iana.org/ gtld/gtld.htm.

- Country-code Top Level Domains (ccTLDs) include **dot.uk**, which is regulated by Nominet at www.nic.uk. Foreign ccTLDs are being used by some businesses: **.it** (Italy) by some IT companies; **.md** (Moldova) by doctors in the US; and **.to** (Tonga) for names such as Come.to, Welcome.to etc. The full ccTLD list is at IANA's site www.iana.org/cctld/cctld-whois.htm.

- Second level domains, used with the country codes, include: **.co, .plc, .ltd, .ac** (for academic institutions), **.gov** (public bodies), and **.org** (for not-for-profits). All the .uk second level domains are regulated by Nominet at www.nic.uk.

## Checking and registering domain names

The web's equivalent of the telephone directory is www.whois.net, which lists all domain names with their registration details.

Several sites enable you to check or to register a domain name, for example, www.internic.net, www.netnames.co.uk or www.nic.uk. The site www.nameboy.com suggests alternatives to your chosen name, while www.greatdomains.com values and sells names.

## Dot.com or dot.co.uk?

There are 22 million dot.com names registered worldwide. Out of the total of 33 million top level generic domain names (gTLDs), 35,000 new domain names are registered every day.

Currently, two thirds of UK companies have .co.uk domain names, and one third are dot.coms, according to a survey by Nominet UK. Companies prefer UK names because they show customers that they are a UK business.

Dot.com failures are probably another reason for the preference.

## New domain names: threats and opportunities

Have you thought about choosing one of the new domain name endings? New generic Top Level Domain names are being released from 2001 onwards, having been agreed by ICANN (the Internet Corporation for Assigned Names and Numbers). These allow you a wider choice, given that the supply of .com names has all but run out. But it is not yet clear what profile and credibility the new names will attract in the marketplace.

Have you protected your firm's name ready for the new wave of domain name endings? The expansion of potential domain name endings means you may want to consider registering additional domain names with new endings, parallel to those you already have. This will avoid potential confusion amongst consumers, where there are other businesses with similar names, and may help forestall cybersquatting.

ICANN's complete list is as follows:

.info - www.afilias.com

.biz - www.neulevel.com

.pro - www.RegistryPro.com - intended for professions, it is planned to offer prefixed versions such as .law.pro and .med.pro

.name

.coop

.aero

.museum

Registrars for only the first two names have been accredited by ICANN so far. There is a risk that the new domain names will enable cybersquatters to register the names of established businesses. Registrations for .biz (www.neulevel.com) and .info (www.afilias.com) were opened with a 'sunrise' period until autumn 2001; during the 'sunrise' period, priority for registration was given to applicants who were relevant trade mark owners.

The European Commission is planning a dot.eu domain name. However, a report adopted on 19 June 2001 and a legal opinion raised further questions and the implementation date is not yet decided.

## Unofficial domain name endings

Unofficial domain name endings also available include **.shop**, **.inc**, **.arts**, **.school**, **.church**, **.love**, **.golf**, **.law**, **.auction** and **.agent**. These are provided by www.new.net, outside the international system for regulating domain names. They cost $25 a year.

NewNet domain names work differently from the ICANN approved .com, .co.uk etc. Because these domain names are not internationally recognised, NewNet names exist only as subdomains of the NewNet domain name itself. NewNet uses routing software to divert users from the short published URL (such as www.sods.law) to the full NewNet subdomain (which would be www.sods.law.new.net in this example). However, there are two problems with these names:

- This redirection works only if the user's ISP has registered with NewNet, and so not all internet users will be able to find a NewNet domain.

- ICANN might in future introduce official domain name endings parallel to the NewNet names. If they were to do so, you would need to re-register the name with the official registrar appointed by ICANN.

## Keep your domain name simple

Your domain name represents your online identity, so choose with care:

- Make your domain name short, simple and memorable.

- Avoid hyphens, slashes etc., which might make it more difficult to type accurately.

- Use capital letters if you wish to make your name more readable, as National Express have with their logo www.GoByCoach.com, for example. Internet domain names are not case-sensitive, so customers will be able to visit you even if they get these wrong.

Strategically, you have three choices:

## Choose a descriptive name?

Using a generic term, which describes your business offering, will be easy to remember and help people find you even though they have not come across your name. Examples include www.pets.com, www.business.com, www.fashion.net, www. packaging.co.uk.

There are some difficulties:

- 98 per cent of English words have already been registered as a dot.com domain name.

- Descriptive names are likely to be difficult to register as a trade mark (see below).

## Create a new online brand name for your business?

There are advantages to adopting a distinctive new name or identity altogether, differentiating your online service from your established name and image. These are as follows:

- The appeal to different audiences.

- The distinction from your existing channels for sales etc., enabling you to have different price structures or service levels.

- The protection from risk to your existing reputation, should there be problems with the online service.

Online financial services have adopted this approach. Examples are the Co-op Bank's Smile, the Prudential's Egg, Abbey National's Cahoot and the Halifax's If. So have other corporations such as British Airways with Go.

But there are risks:

- Your existing clientele may not find you easily.

- You will have to spend money to establish your new 'brand'.

- Some new brand names lead to ridicule!

New corporate brand names include: Xansa (was the FI Group); Accenture (Arthur

Andersen); Lattice (British Gas) and Consignia (the Post Office).

## Use your current name?

Your domain name could simply match what people would guess it to be if they already knew your company name. Lots of internet users look online for businesses they already know, simply by typing the business name in the address box in their browser, and trying the most obvious suffixes, .co.uk or .com. This can be faster than using search engines. So a domain name using your existing name will make you easy to find for people who have heard of you.

## 'Non-roman' domain names

Japanese, Chinese, Arabic and Cyrillic script is not currently recognised by the domain system. The ASCII (American Standard Code for Information Interchange) code, used by the internet, recognises only the roman character alphabet, plus numerals. However, technology companies are developing methods of supporting non-roman domain names, although a uniform standard has yet to be established.

## Domain name shortcuts

You can subscribe to keywords at www.realnames.com, which enable people to reach your site by simply typing your business name into their Microsoft Explorer browser address box. 'Realnames' suggest that this avoids the errors and frustration which can occur when trying to spell a complex domain name correctly.

## Multiple domain names?

Are you making the most of your online branding? Multiple home pages with distinctive domain names are being tried by some law firms to help visitors go directly to information relevant to them. The Law Society uses micro-domains extensively, such as www.it.lawsociety.org.uk. Both Hammonds Suddards Edge and Eversheds have a portfolio of domains; Osborne Clarke has www.gamesbiz.com, Mills & Reeve has www.divorce.co.uk.

# Domain name problems and how to avoid or solve them

## Who owns your domain name?

When using a dial-up Internet Service Provider to obtain a low cost domain name, check their terms of business to ensure that:

- the domain name will genuinely belong to you;

- there are no excessive fees payable, should you wish to transfer the domain name to another Internet Service Provider.

## Cybersquatting and other abuses

Domain name abuses can include:

- **Registration** of your business name by a third party as a domain name. In February 2001, the makers of the chocolate spread 'Nutella' obtained a court order preventing use of the name 'Gnutella' by an internet file-sharing protocol.

- **Typo-piracy:** Where the domain name is a misspelling of your own domain name, brand name or trade mark. For example, in June 2001, a US appeal court confirmed an injunction obtained (under the US Anticybersquatting Consumer Protection Act) by Joseph Shields, proprietor of the site www.joecartoon.com, against an internet domain name wholesaler who had registered joescartoon.com, joecarton.com and others.

- **Brandbashing:** The domain name includes unauthorised use of your name on a site which attacks your reputation. A UK example is the protest site www.dixonsonline.com. A US dispute resolution panel refused to hand the name www.MichaelBloombergSucks.com to Michael Bloomberg of Bloomberg Online, because it had been registered by a campaigning group when Mr. Bloomberg became a candidate in the New York Mayoral elections. Other examples of protest sites are www.ihatestarbucks.com and www.stopesso.com. At www.ecomplaints.com, consumers can publicly whinge about companies.

## Solving domain name disputes

WIPO - the World Internet Property Organisation at www.wipo.int - has a Domain Name Administrative Panel which offers a relatively quick and low cost process for arbitrating domain name disputes. Indicators taken into account by the WIPO arbitrator include whether the other party has:

- a domain name identical or confusingly similar to your own;

- no rights or legitimate interests in that business name;

- lack of genuine commercial purpose;

- registered and used the domain name in bad faith;

- a lack of an active web site for their domain name;

- no previous permission from you to use the name;

- acquired the name primarily for the purpose of:

    - selling it to you for an unreasonable amount;

    - damaging your business by blocking your ability to register the name yourself;

    - misleading visitors into thinking that the site is linked to your business.

UK Internet registrar Nominet (which controls .co.uk name endings) is developing an arbitration system similar to WIPO's.

## Protecting your domain name through trade marking

Domain name disputes are regularly resolved in favour of the party who owns a trade mark related to the domain name.

Registering your logo, graphic or name not only protects against unauthorised use or copying generally, but can be helpful if you encounter domain name problems as well.

The following sites provide more information:

- The government's www.intellectual-property.gov.uk offers general advice on all intellectual property issues.

- The Patent Office www.patent.gov.uk handles applications for trade marks (as well as patents for technical inventions and designs). The site includes detailed guidelines on the type of applications that will and won't be accepted.

- The Chartered Institute of Patent Agents www.cipa.org.uk is one of the professional bodies whose members advise on trade mark applications.

# Step 9: Marketing technology

## Summary

Technology impacts on several key marketing issues:

- The wrong animation or 'plug in' software can restrict access to your site and irritate visitors

- You need a database to track contacts and keep in touch with them

- Security systems protect you against problems which may damage your reputation

- Ecommerce packages are a cost-effective off-the-shelf means to provide a new service

- 'Frames' as a format for your web site has disadvantages

- Developing technology will open up new marketing channels

## Technical resources

Online resources for web development, and free software, are widely available on the internet, at sites such as:

http://hotwired.lycos.com/webmonkey

www.freewarefiles.com

www.download.com

www.netmag.co.uk lists others

See also the other resources mentioned in Step 1 on page 17.

## Visually impaired users

Taking account of the needs of your visually impaired customers is not so restrictive as some people would assume, and can result in improved usability that all visitors to the site will appreciate.

## Animation and other 'plug ins'

Technology enables you to create animations, activity and technical effects on your site. But overuse will make your site difficult to use, complicate its look and feel, and irritate visitors.

### Javascript and pop-ups

On some sites as they launch, a box will pop-up in front of the home page - perhaps an advertisement, or a prompt to register as a user. These pop-ups are normally powered by Javascript, and will operate without the user needing any special software 'plug-in' on their own PC.

Anecdotal evidence is that many users find these irritating, and simply close these pop-ups before they fully open, but your internet designer or developer may propose that you use this technology. If you want to find out more, or to download Javascript to use on your site, visit www.javascripts.com, www.webcoder.com, or www.gamelan .com.

## 'Plug-ins'

'Plug ins' add functionality to your site, but require visitors to have the plug-in on their own PC as well. Plug-ins are free to download from the internet, but some people will be reluctant to do so (they may worry about the time it will take to download; what it might do to their PC; and if they're at work, they'll be anxious that doing so will contravene the office IT policy, or they'll expect it to be blocked by the 'firewall' security on the office system).

Examples of 'plug ins' include:

- **Document presentation**: Adobe Acrobat www.adobe.com is widely used for publishing long documents online. Because it is so functional, it is more acceptable to internet users than some other plug-ins.

- **Animation for graphics**: Flash 5 (or the more sophisticated Shockwave, for simulations and games) from www.macromedia.com are popular with designers, but perhaps less so with users. For examples, see Issy Miyake designerwear site www.pleatsplease.com, solicitors www.millergardner.co.uk

or the gallery of effects at www.mediainspiration.com, and Flash 5 sitebuilder community www.moonfruit.com.

- **Sound and video:** Other products are Real Player at www.real.com, Internet Explorer Media Player at www.microsoft.com/windows/windowsmedia and Apple's www.apple.com/quicktime.

### Internet Explorer mouse-overs

Mouse-overs are a simple tool to add life to a site, and to increase the text you can publish on the home page. As the cursor moves across the webpage, hidden text appears. Although these only work for visitors with Microsoft Internet Explorer, this is used by 80 per cent of visitors to the Law Society's web site. The law firm site www.manches.co.uk is a good example of mouse-overs; on the home page, each item in the contents menu for the site has a mouse-over; as your cursor hovers over an item, a text box appears with a summary of what lies behind.

## Databases

A database is necessary if you are to store, handle and use contact information. In Step 12, we review the many different ways to obtain information - especially email addresses - that will help you target potential buyers (see page 103). You will need a database solution that, as far as possible, allows you to combine data from all these different sources in one system.

If your online visitors can register on your web site, you must ensure that your internet service provider has a simple way to provide registration information to you, so that it can be integrated with your in-house database, and used in the same way.

Database options include:

- the simple address book or contacts folder in your email programme on your PC. Don't forget that, through 'Properties' or 'Preferences' (in Microsoft Outlook, right click on the 'Contacts' icon to access this menu) you can set up access for other PC users on the same network, enabling you to pool information;

- standard PC based database or spreadsheet options. Although powerful, these sometimes need careful customising, and appropriate fields being set up, if they are to meet fully your marketing needs;

- dedicated marketing contacts databases, such as 'Maximiser', Act 2000, and Goldmine. Although more costly, these come prepared with all tools you will need to store full personal details, track your contacts with them (including direct mail, meetings, telephone calls), prompt follow-up activity, categorise them for targeting purposes, and generate mailings etc.;

- full Customer Relations Management systems. According to analyst firm IDC, the leading product is www.siebel.com (with 23 per cent of the $6.2bn market worldwide). Others are www.oracle.com, www.avaya.com and www.peoplesoft.com.

## Other back office software

Other 'back office' software used for setting up and operating sites include:

- server software (e.g. Apache, Microsoft Server);

- database tools (eg Oracle, Microsoft SQL);

- 'middleware' - connecting databases to the www (eg Microsoft Active Server Pages, Cold Fusion);

- enhanced navigation tools (eg Java, Microsoft AcitveX);

- email/webform;

- bulletin boards and chatrooms (eg Perl and CGI scripts);

- search engines for the site (Microsoft Server comes bundled with a search engine. More specialised software includes Alta Vista's Search Engine 3 or www.Brightstation.com's Infosort and Muscat products).

## Security

Security lapses by online traders or financial institutions often make the news. Ecommerce relies on consumers' confidence in security, and that will be undermined by any breaches. You'll find guidance on how to reassure consumers on ecommerce sites in Step 5 on page 54.

There is plenty of general information about security issues online. Examples include a free 'Smart guide' at www.businessadviceonline.org; security consultants' site www.counterpane.com; security evaluation at http://grc.com; an IT security vendor's site www.symantec.com.

Security systems you'll need to consider include:

- firewalls:

  - Provides protection from unauthorised external access to your system (usually included in ISP packages).

  - Filters/monitors your staff's use of the internet, preventing their accessing unsuitable sites.

- anti-virus software to identify and bar incoming viruses: www.silicon.com;

- encryption, providing coded transmission of information: see www.verisign .com or www.pgpi.com for examples;

- user authentication.

Security policies and procedures should include the following:

- internal security policy;

- site content management;

- internet access;

- email protocol;

- privacy and data protection: see www.dataprotection.gov.uk and the OECD privacy statement generator at http://cs3-hq.oecd.org/scripts/pwv3/pwhome. htm.

## Ecommerce

There are two main options for ecommerce technology:

- Develop your own bespoke system, using an internet developer.

- Opt for an off-the-shelf package.

All the big IT players have offerings, which include catalogue templates, 'shopping cart' systems, and credit card verification. So too do some of the specialist IT providers serving particular industry sectors. See www.actinic.com, IBM's home page Creator www.ibm.com/hpc/uk, www.oracle.com, internet service provider www.clara.net, Hewlett Packard www.hp.com and BT's www.bt.com/storecentre for example.

Credit card payments can be handled by specialist online payment processing companies such as www.netbanx.com and www.worldpay.com, which may offer more flexible services than high street banks.

## Frames

Frames split up the screen into separate elements. Your site can be set up so that a menu remains on screen all the time, framing different content as the visitor moves around the site. This can help ease of navigation. Some sites have more complicated set-ups with each element having separate scroll bars.

Disadvantages of frames include the following:

- Links from your site to third party sites may operate so that your site's frame remains around the content of the third party's site. The search engine www.askjeeves.co.uk works in this way. This may create the appearance that you are passing off the other site's content as your own (this was the issue in the Shetland Islands case. In January 2001, news broke over a dispute between publisher Haymarket, and BP Amoco, whose www.castrol.com site linked to Haymarket content within its frame's set-up).

- Search engines have difficulty in collecting information from framed pages (although these problems can be reduced by publishing a 'splash' page to carry the necessary information; live visitors click somewhere on the page to reach the main site and its frames).

- Bookmarks/favourites cannot easily be attached to individual pages within a site, making it more difficult for visitors to record and return to specific information that they found useful.

- Visually impaired people cannot use framed sites easily.

# Delivery channels

The internet of the World Wide Web represents only one delivery channel. Technical developments (although slowed by the dot.com crisis and the anxieties about recession) are likely in the near future, which will open up new marketing channels.

## iTV- interactive television

Accessing the web through your television set is an example of converging technologies - a single appliance able to deliver more and more functions. Interactive television also offers video on demand, electronic programming guides, choice of camera angles, interaction with quiz shows and other programmes, networked games and pause/rewind features.

A web site intended to be viewed across a couple of metres of living-room would call for different design disciplines from those required for viewing on a PC across a few centimetres of desk. Web sites also have to be written to suit the digital TV operator's technical platform.

What is the state of the market?

- The UK leads the world in iTV implementation. According to research group IDC, around 3.9m British households (16.3 per cent of the total) had access at the end of 2000. Forrester put the figure much higher, at 6.3m (over 25 per cent of all households).

- Sky has closed its 'Open' iTV shopping, banking, and email service. Of 5 million Sky Digital subscribers, only 1.7m had registered for email facilities. iTV retail accounted for only £50m in sales in 2000, mostly travel related.

- But a Cyber Dialogue survey of 1,000 US adults in early 2000 found that 70 per cent had no interest in iTV. Jupiter MMXI found that four out of 10 offline consumers could not think of a single iTV feature in which they were interested.

- Research group Gartner estimates that 15 million people will be accessing the internet through their television by 2003, and Forrester estimates that the market will be worth £18bn across Europe by 2005 (according to *Internet Week* magazine).

- Nationwide, in October 2001, launched its own set top box costing less than £30. This will enable customers to access www.nationwide.co.uk on their televisions, without having to subscribe to one of the digital television channels. Customers can use it to view other web sites, but may have to scroll left and right to view their pages. The Nationwide web site has been redesigned for viewing on this system.

- 'Walled gardens' have been used by UK providers such as Telewest, ITVdigital (formerly Ondigital) and BskyB's 'Open.' These 'walled gardens' do not give web access to viewers. Instead, content providers pay the iTV provider for hosting pages which must be rewritten for the provider's technical platform.

- The government will be encouraging the take-up of digital television, so that it is able to switch off analogue broadcasting. 2010 is the earliest that this will happen and public resistance may delay this considerably. This will release bandwidth for sale, probably worth £20bn.

## Text messaging

Text messaging on mobile phones - Short Message Service, or SMS - has proved overwhelmingly popular for personal use. Nine in ten children under 16 now have a mobile phone, and 96 per cent of them use text messaging. A site www.rabbit-on.com has been launched, enabling people to register to receive text messages from a 'virtual flirt'. BBC television devoted a whole evening to text messaging and the *Guardian* ran a competition for the best text message poem.

Now commercial use is being made of the medium for marketing purposes. It is obviously well suited for reaching the 15- to 24-year-old market:

- The film 'Bridget Jones' Diary' was promoted using text messages.

- Worldpop (the digital marketing company run by ex-Radio 1 DJ Peter Powell) and Orange have provided free text message information, discounts on tickets etc. to Ibiza clubbers, in return for which they received text message 'commercials' as well.

- Law firm Fidler and Pepper www.fidler.co.uk now uses text messages to let clients know when contracts have been exchanged on home sales and purchases.

Commercial programs have now been developed so that text messages can be sent from PCs to mobile phones. Examples of providers are www.desoft.co.uk (software prices start at £25 for individuals) and www.redrock.co.uk (aimed at corporate users, prices start at £395).

## Mobile internet and email

WAP - Wireless Application Protocol - was overhyped, failed to deliver true mobile internet access, and failed to take off commercially.

New standards such as GPRS - General Packet Radio System - are expected to offer a marked improvement. These systems will allow real internet access through advanced mobile phones (these new handsets are not yet commercially available) and through mobile phones connected to PDAs (Personal Digital Assistants) like the Psion or Palm.

The marketing potential of GPRS and similar systems includes the ability to launch ads to a mobile phone as the user passes a particular shop. Other commercial uses include mobile networked gaming.

Sources of further information include these sites:

- The Global Mobile Suppliers' Association www.gsacom.com.

- The Mobile Gaming Interoperability Forum www.mgif.org.

- Information on GPRS www.gsmworld.com.

- Demonstration site www.mywapworld.com.

- Sites like www.buzzed.co.uk offer programs to convert a standard HTML www site to WAP.

# Step 10: Designing the site

## Summary

- The home page should work like a magazine cover, drawing people into the site

- Avoid cluttered and confusing look and feel

- Images and graphics should be relevant and download time minimised

- Ease of navigation is vital

- Visually impaired users can and should be catered for

## First impressions

You never get a second chance to make a first impression, so you have to get your home page right.

Internet visitors are impatient, intolerant and fickle, so capture their attention from the outset, before they're off somewhere else.

Their experience of the web site will create perceptions of your products. If the web site is hard to navigate, clumsy, slow to download and has a poor appearance, the customer will assume that your products and services are no better.

'Usability' is an internet essential. A growing body of research and experience shows that too many customers abandon online transactions because of poor usability. No business can afford disaffected customers and lost business. For a good example of a well-designed site, visit the web usability guru Jakob Nielsen's site www.useit.com, which offers tips (as well as plugs for his book).

## Designing the home page

Here are some guidelines:

- **Style:** Use newspaper-style headlines to grab attention. Don't cram it with narrative text. The home page should tempt or intrigue, play to people's worries, or to their self-interest, so that visitors are drawn into the site because they want to know more. Look how one law firm Mills & Reeves's site www.divorce.co.uk does this; www.pampers.com also has also been given the feel of a magazine.

- **Content:** Centre on the visitor and their problems - not yourself. Try starting with a description of an imaginary visitor, their lifestyle and what they'd like from your web site. Don't just list your products, departments or your services. Avoid descriptions of the business's history. Talk about results and use case studies to show how your products and services help customers with their lives or businesses.

- **Format:** Remember that visitors are reluctant to scroll down, so make sure all the important information will be displayed on the screen. Maximise the useful area and minimise the space taken up by navigation aids.

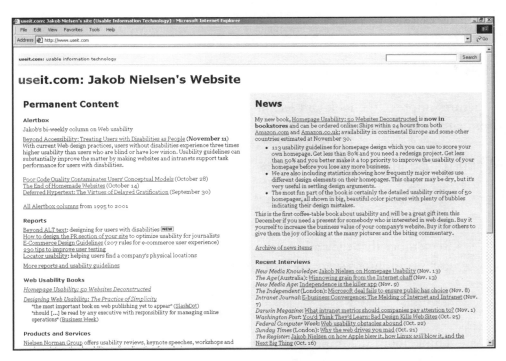

Usability will help differentiate your site from others - Jakob Nielsen is one of the leading exponents

# Look and feel

- Flashing text or repeating animation distract users from content. The satellite television site www.itvdigital.com is such an example.

- Technology can provide animation or mouse-overs which can enhance the visitor's experience, but should be used with care: see Step 9 on technology at 'Animation and other plug-ins' on page 80.

- Frames technology has advantages and disadvantages, which you'll need to consider: see Step 9 on technology at 'Frames' on page 84.

- As with print, avoid mixing too many font styles.

However you design the site, what the visitor sees will depend on: whether they have an Apple Macintosh or a PC; whether they are using Microsoft's Internet Explorer, Netscape or another browser such as Mosaic; and their screen settings. Colour, size and font can all vary. Some users switch all graphics off (to reduce the time it takes a site to load on their machine).

# Pictures and graphics

Pictures improve the look and feel of the home page by breaking up the text - but use them appropriately.

## When to use images and graphics

- Make them relevant. Many sites have pictures of an office building; does this really help?

- Remember that they add to the time it takes to download your site onto the user's computer, especially if the user is on an ordinary telephone line at home.

- People photographs add a human dimension, but don't populate your site exclusively with middle-aged men in suits.

- Think about the impression your pictures create, and think about the people with whom your customers would identify.

- Ensure you have copyright; it is technically easy to copy images from other web sites, but copyright is just as likely to attach to them as to printed images. Some online images contain hidden codes to help detect abuse; where you have commissioned photographs or graphics for printed material from a professional, check whether they have reserved copyright (and the right to a further fee!) for online publication.

## Optimising appearance and download speed

- Avoid publishing titles as an image, otherwise this key information will take too long to appear. Use coloured table cells, for example, to make them stand out.

- Use text at the top and keep images lower down the page to avoid blank spaces as the images wait to load.

- Make sure your web site developer publishes pictures and graphics in as economic a format as possible. Reduce the time images take to download by cropping the picture itself, scaling the image using 'resize' (although not so far that definition is too poor), and compressing the file. Packages such as Adobe Photoshop, Macromedia's Fireworks and Paintshop Pro include programs for optimising images.

- Use ALT tags for each image, so that the visitor can see a description of them, before they download them fully.

- Users can switch off pictures altogether in order to make downloading faster (in the internet explorer toolbar, go to 'view', then 'internet options', then 'advanced'; scroll down to 'multimedia' and uncheck the relevant boxes).

Screen resolution also affects the appearance of your site on visitors' computers. You will have to choose the screen resolution for which your site is optimised. Older or cheaper monitors have lower resolution, for example 640 x 480. Better quality monitors will use higher resolutions 800 x 600 or 1024 x 768. The screen resolution is a measure of the number of 'pixels' (tiny coloured dots) across the screen.

A graphic published on your site will have a fixed number of pixels. It will therefore look larger on a low resolution screen, and smaller on a high resolution display. You can reset the resolution on your own screen to view your site as it will be seen by different visitors.

## User-friendly navigation

Site structure should be kept simple, so that users can reach what they need quickly and easily. The key principles are as follows:

- Design the structure to match the way visitors are likely to seek information; navigation should be intuitive.

- Do not mirror your internal business organisation.

- Test your proposed site structure; for example, write the title of each section on an index card, and lay these out on your desk. Ask other people to check that the plan works.

- Limit the number of levels of menu through which visitors must click, especially if links don't lead to anything substantive, but only to brochure blurb.

Navigation aids can include:

- Your logo or business name on every page so visitors know where on the web they are (because of the way the web works, people may arrive at pages deep within your web site, without seeing the home page).

- 'Trail of breadcrumbs/pebbles' showing where the visitor is in your site's hierarchy (for example: Home ®  Our services ®  International ®  Brussels Office ®  Staff profiles).

- Clear heading (and HTML meta-title) for each page of your site.

- Menu headings in visitors' language - not jargon or technical language.

- Navigation buttons on every page, such as:

    - back to top of the page;

    - back to previous page in the site;

    - back to the home page.

- A site plan outlining the structure and location of key information.

- A-Z list of contents or services.

- A flow chart showing key stages of a process with links to full information.

- 'Our top ten pages' feature.

- Finally, you will have to choose whether or not to use frames technology, which can aid navigation but which has compensating disadvantages: see Step 9.

## Other usability tips

- Make it easy for visitors to print out information - for easier reading offline.

- Include email addresses and other contact information throughout the site, not just on the home page.

## Visually impaired users

It's easier than you might think to design your site so that it meets the needs of visually impaired users. Guidance and a checklist are included at Appendix 2.

There is a strong business case for addressing the issue. Catering for this audience will demonstrate your inclusiveness and enhance your reputation. And there are direct commercial benefits:

- Improved usability will help all visitors to your site.

- There is a market out there. In the UK alone, people with disabilities represent over 15 per cent of the population, with a combined spending power of approximately £50bn. In total, there are two million people with serious sight problems.

- The 1995 Disability Discrimination Act requires goods and services to be made accessible to people with disabilities, and many people interpret this to include web sites.

If you are rebuilding or extending your web presence, why not make use of the free practical guides to help ensure accessible design? Online resources include the following:

- Guides at www.rnib.org.uk/digital and www.w3.org/WAI (site of the Web Access Initiative), the British Computer Society at www.bcs.org.uk and, finally, www.ability.co.uk.

- At www.cast.org/bobby, you can test your site for compliance with accessibility standards.

- The Employers' Forum on Disability at www.employers-forum.co.uk has published the 'Accessible Website Guide' with both practical step-by-step guidance and technical advice.

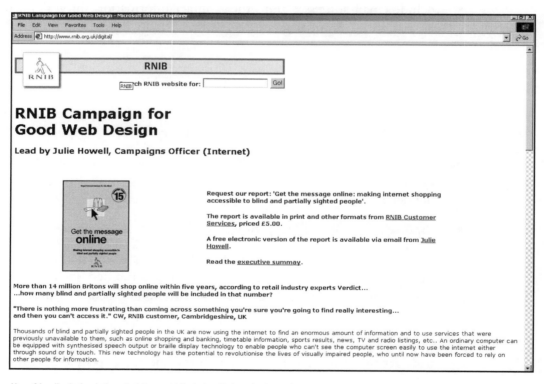

User-friendly design helps all visitors, not just visually impaired people

- At www.guidedogs.org.uk you will find a web site designed for visually impaired users, and you'll see it is as attractive and effective as any other. Incidentally, it includes simulations to show what people with different impairments can see.

## Design resources

For further information on books and sites offering guidance on design and technical issues, please refer to page 11.

# Step 11:  Risk management

## Summary

- Ensure that all features on your site are tested and continually checked

- Do be careful not to pass off another person's site as your own

- If you are maintaining data on individuals, you must register with the Data Protection Registrar

- If you are selling online to customers abroad, there are regulations you must comply with

- Have you protected your domain name?

## Test everything

- Ensure all price information is correct, in case you are held contractually liable to sell goods at a wrongly quoted price.

- Check your site regularly, to ensure it is up to date, and that there are no technical glitches.

- Before launching a new site, an upgrade or new service, you should make sure every link and feature works. Check all the documents are there. Look for typos, especially in headlines, menus and other highly visible content.

- Your contract with your web site designer/developer/consultant should make acceptance of the completed work, signing off the project, and payment of fees, subject to satisfactory completion of testing by you.

- A detailed written 'test pack' is ideal. This should methodically go through your site's main content and features (based on the project deliverables specified in the original contract), and specify the sample checks to be carried out, and the results to be expected. Whoever carries out the tests then records the actual results in the pack.

## Monitor your site's functionality

- Remotely check logistics of your site at www.web sitegarage.com.

- Monitor your site's availability using a service such as www.netwhistle.com.

- Check for broken links, download time etc. with sites such as www.net mechanic.com.

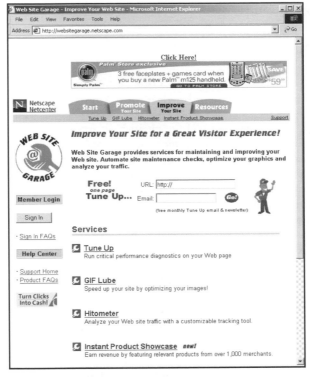

Online services can check that your website is working efficiently

Website Garage web site © 2001 Netscape Communications Corporation. Screenshot used with permission.

## Check for legal compliance

A number of legal web sites offer standard contractual documents for purchase and free guidance. These include www.briffa.com, www.out-law.com, www.desktoplayer .co.uk, www.eversheds80.com, www.lawrights.co.uk and www.infolaw.co.uk, or in the US www.findlaw.com. The best place for finding solicitors to match your needs is the Law Society's www.solicitors-online.com.

## Links to third party sites

Links from your site to third party sites may operate so that your site's frame remains around the content of the third party's site. Be careful not to create the appearance that you are passing off the other site's content as your own, as this can lead to legal disputes.

### Could you be sued abroad?

Websites are global; laws and enforcement are local. *The Economist* in a feature entitled 'The internet's new borders' (11 August 2001) observes:

Long, long ago in the history of the internet…it was widely believed that the internet would help undermine authoritarian regimes, reduce governments' abilities to levy taxes, and circumvent all kinds of local regulation. The internet was a parallel universe of pure data, an exciting new frontier where a lawless freedom prevailed. But it now seems that this was simply a glorious illusion. For it turns out that governments do, in fact, have a great deal of sovereignty over cyberspace. The internet is often perceived as being everywhere yet nowhere, as freefloating as a cloud, but in fact it is subject to geography after all, and therefore to law…Since the internet consists of data sitting inside computers that are located in the real world, it turns out that legal action can be taken - and is being taken - against internet access-providers and publishers, using old-fashioned laws, in old fashioned courts.

Examples to bear in mind include the following:

- **Ecommerce:** Legal requirements for completing online transactions will vary from one country's jurisdiction to another. The subscription service www.next law.com from solicitors Clifford Chance provides online advice.

- **Financial services:** Most countries (including the UK) have tightly regulated regimes for selling financial services. The subscription service www.blueflag.com from solicitors Linklaters provides online advice.

- **Unsuitable material:** The internet portal Yahoo!, which includes an auction site, was ordered by a French judge in November 2000 to find a way to ban French users from purchasing Nazi memorabilia from the site, because this was in breach of French law. In some Islamic countries, the categories of unsuitable material are likely to be wider.

## Data Protection and Privacy

The 1984 Data Protection Act covered personal data held electronically. The 1998 Act extends the law to cover paper files.

If you are maintaining data on individuals:

- you must register with the Data Protection Registrar;

- there are restrictions on how you use the data, and on its disclosure to third parties; normally, you must have peoples' informed consent;

- data must be processed fairly and lawfully. You must ensure you hold only data that is relevant and accurate, and that it is not kept longer than necessary;

- you must have safeguards to prevent unauthorised use;

- there are special rules about 'sensitive' personal data (on racial origin, religious belief, union membership, offences etc.);

- individuals have the right of access to the data you hold on them (subject to payment of a modest fee) and to have corrections made.

Full information about your responsibilities is at the government watchdog site www.dataprotection.gov.uk. Other resources include the following:

- The OECD has a system to help you write a privacy statement at http://cs3-hq.oecd.org/scripts/pwv3/pwhome.htm.

- A tool which informs internet users when a site host is monitoring, released by UK watchdog the Privacy Foundation, is at www.bugnosis.org.

- The site www.cookiecentral.com monitors the use of 'cookies' hidden by some web sites on people's PCs, and which collect information about the individual.

## Distance selling requirements

Businesses which sell goods and services to consumers online must comply with regulations designed to protect consumers and to give them confidence in using 'distance selling' channels.

The Consumer Protection (Distance Selling) Regulations 2000 came into force on 31 October 2000 (the full text is available online at the UK government site www.legislation.hmso.gov.uk/stat.htm). These regulations implement a European Directive, and so similar provisions will apply throughout the EU.

Note these points about the scope of the regulations:

- 'Distance selling' includes the sale of goods or services to consumers on the internet, digital television, mail order, catalogue shopping, phone and fax.

- Business-to-business contracts are not covered; the regulations are primarily designed to help individual buyers.

- Financial services are not covered either; there is separate EU directive on this subject in draft.

- Food and drink, transport, accommodation etc. are also excluded from some aspects of the regulations.

The key requirements of the regulations parallel good practice which many internet traders already follow. As summarised by the news service provided by solicitors at www.eversheds80.com, these requirements are as follows:

- Clear information about the goods or services must be offered to consumers before they are purchased.

- Details required include identity of the supplier, their address (in the case of payment in advance), the price (including taxes), any delivery costs, arrangements for fulfilment etc.

- After a purchase, the consumer must be sent confirmation of the relevant information in writing (this can include fax or email).

- The consumer must be given a 'cooling off period', during which they can cancel their order, of at least seven working days.

- Unless otherwise agreed, distance contracts must be fulfilled within 30 days.

## Security

A range of security issues can affect your web site. For details, see Step 9 about technology on page 82.

## New domain names: threats and opportunities

Have you protected your firm's name ready for the new wave of domain name endings? The expansion of potential domain name endings means you may want to consider registering additional domain names with new endings, parallel to those you already have. This will avoid potential confusion amongst consumers where there are other businesses with similar names, and may help forestall cybersquatting.

New generic Top Level Domain ('gTLD') names are being released from 2001 onwards, having been agreed by ICANN (the Internet Corporation for Assigned Names and Numbers). See Step 8 on Domain Names on page 71 for more details.

## Ecommerce risks

If you are planning ecommerce activity, consider the following risks:

- The 'five nines' ideal: What will it cost you to run a web site that is 99.999% reliable?

- 'Cannibalisation': Will your online commerce adversely affect any existing revenue streams? How will your pricing strategy be affected? Will online comparison shopping force you to offer lower prices, and what will be the effect on profit?

- 'Channel conflict': How will your sales force, distributors, agents, and the shops you supply, react when you sell direct on line?

- Can you deliver (1): Take care to avoid becoming contractually committed to provide something that you cannot supply. Check that prices are correctly quoted, and that references to special offers are deleted when they have expired. Make clear any geographical limitations on your ability to fulfil orders.

- Can you deliver (2): Do you have robust fulfilment and delivery systems that can reach customers wherever they've come from worldwide? Many dot.coms have failed to get this right. As *The Economist* pointed out in a dot.commerce special issue (26.2.00):

  > Physical shoppers, after all, handle their own order fulfilment, by choosing the goods and paying for them at the checkout, as well as their own delivery, by personally taking them home. And they do all this at their own expense, in both time and money.

- 'Legacy' systems: How will you integrate your web orders and customer information with your existing legacy systems, whether paper or IT based?

- Ensuring that your customers will have the confidence to trade online (see Step 5 and the ecommerce model on page 44).

# Step 12: Promotion and communication

## Summary

- Don't forget offline marketing
- Use all the web's opportunities to gather market intelligence
- Email is one of the most effective marketing tools
- Collect email addresses methodically
- Try newsgroups and chatrooms
- Establish mutual links with other web sites
- Consider online advertising
- Consider entries to relevant online directories
- Offer online customer incentives
- Develop online press relations activity
- Enter your site for competitions and awards
- Set your site up to be search-engine friendly
- Submit your pages to search engines regularly

For many people, the term 'marketing' only refers to the activity discussed in this step: promoting your site to the market. In fact, as well as the strategy and planning stages in Steps 1-4, the marketing mix involves all the issues about product, price, place, people, resources etc. dealt with in Steps 5-11.

## Don't forget offline marketing

Offline marketing for your site is as important as online marketing, and the mix can include:

- Press releases - Encourage journalists to use your web site as a source of authoritative comment on issues affecting your business sector.

- Direct mail - to your customer database.

- Your firm's - newsletter should keep referring readers to the site for more information.

- Advertising.

- All office stationery must give your www address - letterhead, your brochure, business cards.

- Directory entries.

## Marketing intelligence

The internet provides many opportunities for 'passive' marketing: gaining intelligence about your customers, markets and competitors that you can use to plan and improve marketing activity, your web site, and your products and services themselves. Possibilities include:

- Checking up on competitors' web sites (in research done by the Law Society, solicitors said that this was their most frequent purpose for using the internet!).

- Visiting chatrooms and newsgroups (explained below), protest or consumer retaliation sites (examples are www.dixonsonline.com, www.regvardy.co.uk, www.ihatestarbucks.com and www.stopesso.com; at www.ecomplaints.com, consumers can publicly whinge about companies) and consumer organisations (such as the Office of Fair Trading, Consumers' Association and National Consumer Council). Here, you can read what consumers say is wrong with your competitors and their products, or what needs they have which they would like to be addressed.

- Monitoring statistics, emails and comments generated by your own site, as described in Step 14 on page 130.

- Reviewing audience trends, statistics and surveys published on the market research sites listed in Step 1 on page 17.

## Make the most of email

### Low cost and effective

Email is a low cost and flexible marketing tool. It avoids the costs and lead-times involved in printing and fulfilling conventional direct mail, and you can reach targeted individuals at their desks.

The online advertising agency DoubleClick believes that email marketing is likely to become more important than banner advertising; *Internet Magazine* in October 2001 reported that in the three months to June, DoubleClick had sent out two billion emails on behalf of 250 clients.

## Email marketing techniques

The Fabulous Bakin' Boys are muffin makers based in Witney. According to a case study in the *Guardian*'s 'Small Business Solutions' (4 October 2001), they published a database of jokes at their web site www.bakinboys.co.uk and encouraged visitors to email them to friends and colleagues. The company also emails irreverent advertising with links back to their web site, which now includes online games, such as Cake Invaders. Business is growing by 30 per cent to 40 per cent a year.

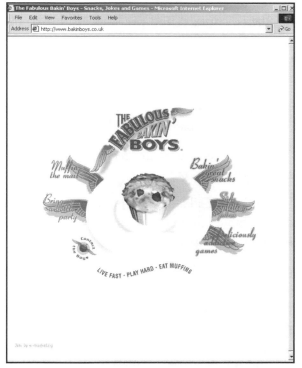

Encourage viral marketing – visitors emailing their friends about your site

These suggestions will help you make the most of the medium:

- Marketing emails require at least as much preparation as other marketing communications. You have only a few seconds in which to gain the recipient's attention, so the heading and first line or two are crucial. Well-written copy is essential and there must be a simple and attractive way for interested recipients to take another step, for example, clicking on a link back to your web site. For more help, see Appendix 1.

- Build selling into emailed order acknowledgements, invoices, receipts etc., for example, with related product news and links back to your web site.

- Make sure everyone in your business uses a standardised signature block in their outgoing emails. All emails sent out by the firm should include standard information about the firm, including contact details and the internet domain name.

- Email news - about special offers, new or improved products or services, discount schemes, technical changes, key staff appointments, expansion plans etc. - to your clients, contacts and previous visitors to the site helps to build customer loyalty. Always include the web address of relevant pages on your site, which the recipient can click on to obtain more information, encouraging people to return to the site.

- Include email addresses or forms on individual pages throughout your web site, as well as at the home page. This will encourage contact with you.

- Use 'viral' marketing, encouraging recipients of emails to forward your message to their own contacts.

- As the 'sender', and in email addresses published on your web site, use named contacts such as abida@ rather than anonymous addresses such as sales@, because these sound more personal.

- In promotional emails, tell recipients of your regular emails how they can remove themselves from your circulation list.

## Be aware of the risks

'Spamming'- the inappropriate mass circulation of promotional email - breaches 'netiquette', the informal code that governs the internet. The response from recipients can be very hostile, so avoid abusing the system. The standard guide to netiquette is published at www.rfc1855.org.

Other disadvantages of email include the following:

- People's inboxes are often so busy they will simply delete marketing messages after reading only the title.

- Programs can be set up on individual PCs or on company email systems to delete 'junk' email.

- There is less opportunity to make an impact with graphic design or colour. Some recipients will lack the software to open graphics; dial-up users will find that your email takes several frustrating minutes to download to their inbox. You could offer recipients the option to sign up for an enhanced version of the newsletter with pictures or graphics in an email newsletter (as does www.economist.com).

## Anticipate responses

Plan ahead when launching an email campaign. Have you got the resource to handle the volume of replies, enquiries and orders?

Senders regard email as an instantaneous medium and will expect a reply, or at least an acknowledgement, within a day, so have systems to ensure you are able to respond quickly. Prepare FAQs (answers to frequently asked questions) so that a range of model email replies and responses to telephone enquiries is available.

## How to collect email addresses

Maximise use of your internet site, email and other communications to gather contact data, which you can use to encourage return visits to the web site.

Virgin Wines ran a promotion campaign, now notorious, which included a competition. Entrants were required to provide email addresses for three other people, as part of their competition entry. Virgin Wines built up an email database much more rapidly than would have otherwise been possible.

Data protection and other legislation imposes some restrictions on how you collect and handle information, so check Step 11 on Risk Management (page 97) to make sure that your activities meet legal requirements.

There are several ways to obtain information about individual visitors (as opposed to anonymised statistics):

- Encourage visitor registration on your web site itself: Most internet users think registration is time-wasting, unless they're sure they'll get something valuable in return there and then (Masons at www.out-law.com ask you to register in order to download articles, for example).

- Consider using 'cookies' that automatically capture data from visitors. Cookies are text files that your site can leave on a visitor's computer. Your site can then track an individual's progress through your site, and recognise a repeat visitor. However, if you use cookies, you will need to explain this in your Privacy Policy, and you will need to allow users to withhold information in order to meet concerns about data protection and privacy. Visit www.cookiecentral.com, for example.

- Buy email lists from an agency. But check how these have been gathered. Have the Data Protection requirements been followed? Have people listed opted-in (ticked a box explicitly agreeing to their details being made available to other companies); or is it an opt-out list (it is assumed that people have no objection to their details being passed on, unless they have ticked a box to withhold permission)? If you don't take these precautions, you may find that recipients of your email object to a breach of their privacy.

Obvious ways to collect email addresses, missed by many businesses, are as follows:

- Save email addresses from incoming emails.

- Include space for email addresses in order forms etc.

- Request email addresses from telephone enquirers, personal callers.

## Newsgroups and chatrooms

There are several types of virtual forum where internet users 'meet' to exchange news and information:

- **Web sites** such as www.beme.com and www.confetti.com offer chatrooms and bulletin boards to their visitors. So do many community and campaign sites.

- **AOL** and other internet portals also provide chatrooms. You can access these only if you are a member.

- **Usenet newsgroups** are a separate internet system. Each of the 60,000 or so newsgroups have their own theme, and allow participants to post messages that everyone in the group can read. Your internet access provider probably offers a news server which you can set up in the newsreader program that is part of Netscape, Microsoft Explorer or other browsers. Alternatively, you can reach the Usenet Newsgroups through an ordinary web site such as www.deja.com. *The Rough Guide to the Internet* and similar publications tell you more about how the system works and provides listings of some of the busiest newsgroups.

- **Live chatrooms** using Internet Relay Chat (IRC) or similar systems. Find

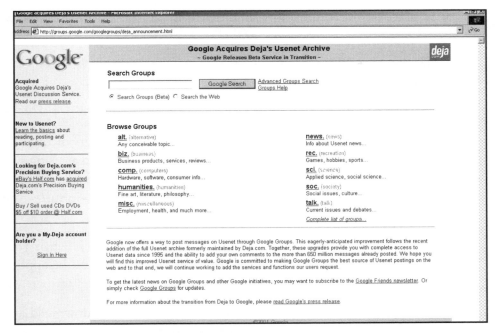

Newsgroups have real potential if used sensitively

© Google Brand Features are trade marks of Google Inc.

more information on how this works, together with channel listings, at a site such as www.irchelp.org/irchelp/networks or again through publications such as *The Rough Guide to the Internet.*

All these services, used with care, can help your marketing. Begin by finding the online discussions used by your audiences. You then have the following opportunities:

- You can post helpful comments or information in answer to questions or discussions that are being posted.

- Read what consumers say is wrong with your competitors and their products. Use this information as the basis for your promotion (not through the newsgroup) of the contrasting advantages of your own.

- Use postings to improve your understanding of your customers and their problems, and use this intelligence in planning your strategy, or writing your marketing communications, or in refining your products and services.

It is important to avoid explicit marketing messages, since they would be regarded as an abuse of the forum. This could result in damage to the image of your business.

## Advertising online

### How can you advertise online?

- **Email newsletters:** Find out whether your customers or other key audiences subscribe to any email newsletters. Many carry advertising, and will often target niche markets, making them ideal for focused advertising. Listings of e-zines can be found at www.meer.net/~johnl/e-zine-list/ and www.factsheet5.com.

- **Banner or pop-up advertising on web sites:** This is when your advertising message is published on another web site. 'Filters' can be applied so that it is seen only by specified types of visitor to the web site, to increase targeting.

- **Affiliation or co-branding:** For example, you can download a search facility from Amazon so that visitors to your site can look for books and other products; and you receive a percentage of the sale price.

As well as banners, some sites include 'pop-up' advertisements, which appear in front of a web page as the page launches in the visitor's browser.

- Some industry commentators suggest that these are more effective because the visitor cannot simply ignore the 'pop-up', but must, at the minimum, click to close it.

- However, many users find these irritating and simply close these pop-ups before they fully open. If you want to find out more, or to download Javascript to use on your site, visit www.javascripts.com, www.webcoder.com or www.gamelan.com.

For more help with writing advertising, see Appendix 1.

## Is it value for money?

- **Interactive?** Internet users can click on a banner there and then for further information or to take further action. This immediacy cannot be achieved by print advertisements, for example. But many internet users simply ignore or block internet ads.

- **Targeted?** By selecting the right web sites, pages or keyword searches to carry your banner, you can ensure you reach only those people most likely to respond positively. But what proportion of your target audience are actually using those pages or functions?

- **Effective?** People now use the internet with more purpose than in the mid-90s when it was first introduced. They are more interested than ever in content and less likely to be distracted by links irrelevant to the main task of their internet session.

## Why has internet advertising disappointed?

Since 2000, banner advertising on the web has been losing credibility and this is demonstrated by the 16 per cent drop in Yahoo's advertising revenue in that year. Despite this, projections from eMarketer, Jupiter and DataMonitor project continuing growth of online advertising spend in Europe.

*The Economist* analysed the online advertising market in a feature 'Banner ad blues' (22 February 2000) and concluded that:

> The immediate problem is simple: too many pages and too few advertisers…as a result… the amount that remaining advertisers are willing to pay is falling to as little as $1 per thousand views (a measure known as CPM), down from ten times that a couple of years ago.

However, *The Economist* does note that web advertising is still in its infancy as the first internet advertisements ran just six years ago. It represents only 3 per cent of all advertising, and five of the world's top ten advertisers, which collectively spend billions of dollars each year on traditional advertising, spent less than $1m each in 2000 online advertisements.

Financial and other data on current online marketing trends can be found at the New Media Age magazine site http://omega.nma.co.uk/adstats.asp, at www.emarketer.com/analysis/eadervertising and elsewhere.

A www.FT.com feature on 2 March 2001 identified a number of special factors explaining its decreasing popularity:

- **Banners are boring:** Compared to television advertising, for example, they are unsophisticated and little creative effort is put into developing them. They have been easy for users to ignore.

- **Performance** - or lack of it - is easy to measure. The number of internet users who see a banner advertisement and click through to the product information is typically 0.5 per cent - 2 per cent. Response rates to magazine advertisements or outdoor posters could be as low, but reliable statistics are much harder to come by. Lord Lever famously remarked that he knew that half of the money he spent on advertising was wasted, but he didn't know which half. With internet advertising, paradoxically, the lack of immediate direct response is transparent.

- **Software programmes** are available which can filter out banner advertising (these include AdSubtract, AdWiper, AdFilter, Internet Junkbuster Proxy, WebWasher and www.guidescope.com).

- **Expectations were high:** Many dot.com business models were founded on the assumption that free-to-use services could be funded entirely by advertising revenue. Up to the end of 1999, this belief was fuelled by the sums spent by dot.coms themselves, in order to build up their customer bases. When these expectations proved unrealistic, disillusionment set in.

- **Economic downturn:** Fears during 2001 about impending recession have led to reductions in advertising spend generally.

## How to plan your banner advertising campaign

If you do decide to undertake a banner advertising campaign, Richard Dennys of the SIFT Group explained in the magazine of the Professional Services Marketing Group, how you can make it a success. His tips included some of the following:

1. **Research where to purchase advertising space:** Who is the typical prospect for your product or service? Browse the search engines, directories and industry-specific sites to see which sites cater for your target audience. Look out for competitors' banner advertising. Decide which sites look the most appropriate.

2. **Ask for site statistics:** You need to be sure that the site really is visited by sufficient numbers of the people you wish to reach. Contact the sites you have selected to obtain the relevant data. Numbers of 'hits' may be impressive but can be misleading; you should obtain statistics for unique visitors and as much information about their demographics as possible. Look for ways to verify statistics: some sites now have the Audit Bureau of Circulation auditing their web site statistics.

3. **Obtain pricing information:** Ask for a banner rate card, giving you a list of prices and placement options. Costs will be quoted as:

   - 'CPM' meaning 'cost per thousand impressions': The price you pay will be based on the number of visitors to the site who have merely seen the advertisement.

   - 'CTR' meaning 'cost per thousand click-throughs': The price will be based on the number of visitors who actually click on your advertisement, in order to see your more detailed information.

   Costs can be as much as £90 per thousand clicks for premium sites, down to £5 per thousand for non-specific ad opportunities. They are often sold in bulk by agencies such as ValueClick and FlyCast. Ask about any discounts or packages available, for example, for an extended run.

4. **Check how your banner will appear:** You will need to discuss and agree:

- which page will feature your banner, and where on the page it will be;

- whether your banner will have an exclusive run (and so will always appear in that space) or will rotate (so that your banner will alternate with others);

- if rotating, how often will they rotate;

- whether you will share the page with other banners.

5. **Ask about banner submission guidelines:** Technical constraints may be tight. Important things to find out about are: maximum file size; allowable file formats (GIF, HTML, Flash, javascript etc.); dimensions in pixels and any design restrictions. The Internet Advertising Bureau www.iabuk.net, a trade group for web publishers, has voluntary guidelines for advertising formats.

6. **Administration:** Confirm:

- Submission deadlines.

- Lead time between submission and publication online.

- When your banner will begin and end its run.

- Access to statistical reports, what will be provided, how frequently and how quickly they will be issued.

7. **Get it in writing:** Ensure there is a written contract dealing with all these issues.

8. **Design the banner:** You will need to be imaginative if you are to attract and keep browsers' interest!

## Online directories

Online directories proliferated before the dot.com crisis, offering listings in portal sites that would be heavily promoted and would become first port of call for large numbers of potential customers. However, in too many instances, the promised traffic failed to materialise.

Despite these failings, directory entries should still be considered, but you should approach possibilities in the same methodical way as for online advertising. Do beware of committing too much money without hard proof of visitor numbers!

Business directory possibilities include:

- Local and regional press directories, some independent, others as part of the Fish4 series.

- Business Links and Chamber of Commerce listings.

- Local authority business development listings.

- Other local online services: You can locate these by doing an internet search on the name of your town.

- Trade, industry or professional bodies (the Law Society's www.solicitors-online.com is becoming the pre-eminent UK internet legal directory).

- Specialist portals serving your prospective clients.

## Mutual links and banner exchanges

Mutual links to and from other sites sharing your interests (but not competing!) are a possibility. Contact other businesses directly to negotiate mutual links or you can try one of the online banner exchange services, such as:

www.webring.org.

www.linkexchange.com, now part of MSN's www.bcentral.com.

www.advertwizard.com.

Find which sites already link to your own by typing 'Link to' in your browser's address box, followed by your domain name.

## Customer incentives

Summer 2001 has the seen the demise of some of the online customer incentive schemes, which attempted to apply the Co-op Dividend or Green Shield Stamp approach to the internet:

- Beenz: Online traders offered customers 'Beenz' points for each purchase.

Customers could collect these in an online account, and redeem them when making future purchases from participating sites.

- Flooz: Provided web-based gift certificates, which could be redeemed at about 30 web sites, including Barnes & Noble and Tower Records.

However, www.mypoints.co.uk and www.ipoints.co.uk continue to offer traders the opportunity to affiliate, so that visitors and buyers at their web site can gain points, which can then be redeemed against further online purchases.

## Press relations online

Use email to issue press releases:

- **Directories** such as *Willings Press Guide* or the *Guardian's Media Guide* provide listings. Or try www.mediafinder.com.

- **Local and regional newspapers**: There are around 1,400 titles, and nine out of ten people read a regional paper every week. Typically, in a given area, more people read their local paper than read the *Sun*. Many titles are members of the Newspaper Society, which can provide helpful advice on major campaigns.

- **Local and regional radio and TV**: Local radio can be powerful and accessible.

- **Trade journals**: Find out which are read by your customers and other key audiences. Use the media directories or groups such as the Periodical Publishers Association, which includes many business publishers and is at www.b2bmedia.co.uk.

Tips on press releases include the following:

- Emailed press releases should be in plain text with no attachments.

- Head the message 'Press Release' with a self-explanatory title which indicates factually what the story is about.

- The first sentence should answer the questions: who, what, where and when. It should be possible to understand the entire message of the release by reading only the first sentence. The body of the press release can go on to deal with the 'why' - the more detailed explanations.

- Include dates for events. If you don't want the information published before a specific date, include the words 'EMBARGO: not to be published before [time] on [date]'.

- Write the release in the same style used by the media you are targeting (so that it would not appear out of place if reproduced word for word). Keep it brief, no more than a side of A4.

- Content should relate to the interests of the audience; it should not merely tout your product or service. Explain how they can benefit (saving money, saving time, gaining peace of mind, pre-empting problems). Address their self-interest or concern.

- Highlight any facts specific to the local or specialist audience that you intend the piece to reach.

- Before sending a press release, check the deadlines for the paper or programme in which you want coverage - lead times for business supplements in the local press can be longer than you would expect.

- Send your release to the news desk or relevant specialist editor, unless you have been able to identify a named contact.

- At the end, give the name and telephone numbers of the person from whom further information can be sought - and ensure that they are available at the right time to receive any calls!

## Competitions and awards

Success in competitions and awards provides public recognition, participation in the promotion for the scheme itself, together with reward and motivation for everyone involved in your site. A few of the organisers of regular awards are:

- Yellow Pages online: www.yell.co.uk/awards: The online directory runs an annual competition and publishes details of shortlisted and winning sites.

- E-commerce awards: www.ecommerce-awards.co.uk: Organised since 1999 by the agency UKonlineforbusiness (a DTI-led partnership between industry and government) and Interforum, a not-for-profit organisation which helps British business to trade electronically; the site links to a good number of

Awards and competitions provide excellent opportunities for publicity

commended sites, but disappointingly the reasons for their selection are not given.

- Magazines such as www.computerweekly.co.uk, www.prweek.com, Future Publishing's *Internet Advisor* www.uknetawards.co.uk and *New Media Age* www.nma.co.uk run award schemes.

- The *FT* Business Web Site of the Year Awards: www.ft.com/awards.

- The Webbies: www.webbyawards.com: The fifth annual awards ceremony took place in San Francisco in July 2001 (winners' acceptance speeches were limited to just five words!).

- Microsoft's 'Digital Britain' awards launched in 2001: www.microsoft.com/uk/digitalbritain/awards.

- The annual *Internet Business* awards, which began in August 2000 - www.ibmag.co.uk.

- Specialist industry awards schemes (legal IT specialists have the Society for Computers and Law competition www.scl.org; and the LOTIES, the Legal Office Technology Innovation Awards www.inbrief.co.uk; as well as awards offered by magazines such as *Legal IT*).

# Search engines

## How to be search-engine friendly

With the proliferation of internet sites, it is increasingly difficult to ensure that your site will reach the top positions in relevant search results listings. However, you can help your site to be search-engine friendly:

- Publish using HTML - not database systems like ASP or CGI.

- Include key words at the top of the page (e.g. 'Solicitor', 'Accident specialist') and repeat key in the body text.

- Devise meta <TITLE>, <DESCRIPTION> and <KEYWORDS> tags, for search engines to read.

- Hide your graphics.

- Avoid 'Frames' technology.

- Submit your site details to the main search engines and resubmit frequently.

- Consider search engine advertising programmes.

- Look out for XML!

This section looks in more detail at each of these suggestions, but we begin by explaining how search engines work.

## How search engines work

There are at least 400 search engines. These are the main types of search engine:

1. Deep search engines, such as www.altavista.com. These have automated spiders or robots that remotely analyse and index your site. The others are

Infoseek, Excite, Webcrawler, Hotbot, Lycos and Northern Light.

2.  Directory sites, which classify sites into categories. The most thorough is www.yahoo.com, whose staff review every site before it is included.

3.  Meta-search engines, which carry out searches on a range of other internet search engines. Examples are www.dogpile.com, www.askjeeves.com and www.metafind.com.

4.  Intelligent agents such as Autonomy at www.agentware.com, WebCompass at www.qdeck.com, Alexa at www.alexa.com.

Each search engine uses its own algorithms ('rules') for including web pages in their index. These algorithms are continually updated, and are unpublished, so as to reduce 'spamdexing' by unscrupulous webmasters trying to trick search engines into giving their sites undue prominence.

For further information on search engines, one of the best resources is www.searchenginewatch.com. A tutorial and free updates on search engines are available at www.deadlock.com.

## Publish using HTML - not database systems like ASP or CGI

Search engines can read and index each separate page published on the web in 'fixed' HTML but the search engines' web crawlers cannot access information held in online databases. Put simply, they are unable to fill in the form that tells the database what it is looking for. This 'invisible' internet includes patent records, telephone directories, interactive maps, stock prices, census data etc. Chris Sherman, of SearchEngineWatch.com, offers insights to this hidden data in *The Invisible Web: Uncovering information sources search engines can't see.*

Other sites operate using ASP or CGI, which serve fluid content, customised for the visitor. ASP and CGI sites rely on an underlying database, which generates pages of information for individual users as they navigate the site. Again, the web crawlers cannot penetrate beyond the home page of such sites.

*Internet Magazine* (November 1999) quoted www.greatgames.co.uk, which receives 80 per cent of its customers through search engines. The site used Actinic Catalogue, which gives each product a separate HTML page. Founder Adam Reynolds commented:

It's all very well indexing your home page with generic keywords to get round the problem of dynamic page generation. But most customers don't go looking for products using terms like 'games'... Many of them type in[to the search engine] the exact make and model they're looking for...All my matching pages come up.

'Doorway' pages can be created to make dynamically generated sites more search-engine friendly. A tutorial is available at www.searchengines.com/doorway_pages.html.

## Include keywords in your text

Give your page a title, and include keywords describing your business. Repeat title and keywords a few times in body text on the page.

Avoid the following which may lead search engines to exclude your site altogether:

- Over-repetition of keywords.

- Text the same colour as the background colour, intended to be visible to search engines rather than humans.

## Use metatags

'Metatags' are the hidden labels on web pages that tell search engines what the pages are about. They play an important role when a search engine indexes and ranks your search engine in their database (a few, such as www.northernlight.com, do not use the metatags at all).

Getting the metatags right will improve the likelihood that your site will be identified in search results. Make sure each page of your web site has its own individual title, description and keyword metatags.

You can deconstruct the metatags used on nearly any web page by selecting:

- 'View' in the top toolbar of your browser;

- 'Source' from the drop-down menu;

- then a page with the source HTML will launch, showing all the information used by your browser to set the page up.

For search-engine friendliness, the most important metatags are these (found between the <head> tags on your site):

**<title>** The title of the page, the first piece of information used in cataloguing your site. This title will appear in the visitor's browser title bar and in their lists of favourites or bookmarks. Use up to 70 characters to give your business name and describe your business.

**<meta name= 'Description'>** A concise description of the page, which will be displayed in search engine results - and which the user will read when selecting the most relevant or appealing sites to visit. Use up to 25 words or 250 characters.

**<meta name= 'Keywords'>** These words enable search engines to list your site appropriately and to include it in search results when keywords match the search terms that have been used. Use up to 1,000 characters and separate each word with a comma.

You should consider including the following:

- Common misspellings of the keywords you use.

- Phrases of two or three words together, if that's what users might search for.

Keywords should avoid the following:

- The name of a competitor's company or product as legal action could be brought against you.

- Repeating the same word many times.

- Including popular but irrelevant search terms, such as 'Britney Spears'.

Search engines are programmed to detect attempted tricks with keywords, and may ignore the page completely.

Web services such as www.ineedhits.com offer an analysis of your web site's metatags as part of their search engine registration programme.

For more information on metatags, try www.htmlgoodies.com/tutors/head.html.

For information on search engine robots, or spiders, try www.robotstxt.org/wc/robots.html.

Use the 'View source' button on your toolbar to look at the metatags for any website

## Hide your graphics

Graphics cannot be read by search engines and will reduce the relevance of your pages. You can avoid this problem by hiding the graphics, following one of the 'robots exclusion' protocols. Your site will include a robots.txt file, with instructions to the search engine robot telling it what not to read on the site. For information on these protocols, try www.robotstxt.org/wc/robots.html.

## Avoid frames

See Step 9 on technology for an explanation of frames, and a discussion of their advantages and disadvantages.

## Register your site with the search engines

### The most popular search engines

Check www.searchenginewatch.com for the most up-to-date statistics on search engines. In July 2001, the site reported Jupiter MMXI's findings and these were as follows:

- Yahoo 61.4 per cent
- MSN 56.5 per cent
- AOL 40 per cent
- Lycos 28.8 per cent
- Go/Infoseek 21.7 per cent
- Netscape 20.2 per cent
- Excite 15 per cent
- Google 14 per cent
- NBC 13 per cent
- Ask Jeeves 12 per cent

### How to register on search engines

All the search engines offer you the opportunity to 'Submit a Site', 'Suggest a Link', 'Register your URL' or similar. There will be pages with guidelines, terms of service, background information and a submission form:

- Usually, you will find a link at the foot of the search engine's home page which will take you to a submission form.

- Yahoo! and AOL are different: You must first search the site directory to find the category which is most appropriate for your site (for example, Law Pack's site www.lawpack.co.uk was listed at Yahoo under → regional → countries → United Kingdom → business & economy → shopping & services → law).

The following information is normally requested when submitting a site:

- URL and site title: This should be the official business name for a commercial site.

- Your contact details.

- Description of the site - a brief readable sentence (perhaps no more than 25 words).

- Other key words.

Clear objective language is requested 'to help our editors evaluate your site', and you are often asked to avoid 'promotional language' (the best, the coolest, the number one, etc).

Submission policies are published on most search engine sites and typically cover the following:

- Submit your site only once.

- Good quality sites are preferred: Your site must be available 24/7, can load quickly, be user-friendly, be well maintained and updated regularly.

- Substantive, original and credible content should be offered; single page sites are sometimes not listed.

- Links (if provided) should all work and be relevant to content but the site shouldn't consist exclusively of links.

- 'Mirror' sites with identical content but different URLs are not permitted, nor are addresses that 'Redirect' to another address.

- Illegality is not permitted (child pornography, abusive content, copyright infringements).

- Pornographic sites are not listed at all by some search engines, or are restricted to 'Adult' areas in others.

- Sites 'under construction' will not be listed.

According to www.ineedhits.com, the lead times for search engine inclusion are as follows:

- 1-2 weeks: AltaVista, Infoseek (Go Network).

- 2-6 weeks: Excite, HotBot, Lycos, Webcrawler.

- 8-12 weeks: Yahoo.

Some search engines, for a fee of perhaps $200, offer an 'express' programme promising faster registration.

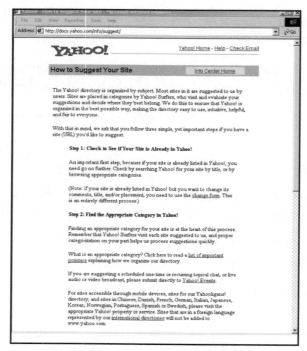

Make the effort to submit your site to the main search engines

© Yahoo

## How long will it take?

Manually submitting your home page to half a dozen key search engines will take at least half a day.

If your site offers a variety of content and services, then submission of only your home page will force you to generalise in your submission to the search engines. For the most effective match to the search terms that people use on search engines, you ought to consider submitting the main pages separately.

## Automated search engine submission

Online services offer to submit your site automatically to 300 or more search engines, including the main search engines. Some offer a basic service free of charge; otherwise the cost can be as little as $10 and packages for less than $50 can also include metatag advice and analysis. Examples include:

- www.ineedhits.com

- www.submit-it.com

- www.exploit.com

- www.looksmart.com (partner sites include AltaVista, Excite, MSN etc)

### Consider search engine advertising programmes

Many search engines offer paid-for promotion opportunities linked to specified search terms. *Internet Magazine* (February 2001) criticised the development of these programmes. For example, www.GoTo.com - which backs search engines such as Lycos, Netscape and AOL in the US, and Freeserve and Ask Jeeves in the UK - auctions search terms on its system to the highest bidder. As a result, a search for 'Tesco' listed 'PriceRunner', a comparative shopping site, first in the list. Type 'Amazon' and the top result is 'Barnes & Noble.'

Advertisers on search engines can be victims of protest campaigns which incur direct costs. For example, in June 2000, the top bidders for top listing in search results for the term 'auto-dialler' were paying GoTo more than $6 for each user to click to them. A campaign was started amongst people irritated by telemarketing, which aimed to encourage consumers to run up auto-diallers' advertising bills, by repeatedly clicking on their search listing. In fact, GoTo commented that the impact of the campaign appeared negligible.

But if you can't beat them, join them!

## Online marketing resources

Online marketing resources include:

- *Adweek* magazine's www.technologymarketing.com.
- The US-based Internet Marketing Centre's www.marketingtips.com.

- *Marketing Magazine*'s online marketing information at www.marketing. haynet.com.

- Sites such as www.clickz.com, with online marketing reviews.

- *Internet Magazine*'s web marketing news at www.internet-sales.com/hot.

- Other magazine sites such as www.mediaweek.com.

# Step 13: Keeping the site up to date

## Summary

- Don't allow your web site to become a cobwebsite!

## Publish regular updates

- Allocate responsibility (e.g. to one of your support staff) to monitor site content and publish information to the site, say once a week.

- Use a spreadsheet to track material published to the site and to log dates when items should be reviewed for currency, replaced or archived.

- Identify key staff to act as content providers, owning areas on the site, and tasked with checking their material and providing new content.

- Help users by dating individual documents.

## Avoid time traps

These traps highlight out of date sites:

- An old 'last updated' date on the Home Page or elsewhere. If you're not publishing to the site very frequently, avoid a date which might make the site look out of date to the first time visitor, even when it might not be.

- 'News' that, well, isn't.

- 'Forthcoming events' information for dates that have gone by.

- Out-of-date phone numbers (e.g. London 0171 and 0181 numbers).

- Hypertext links that no longer work.

# Step 14: Monitoring and evaluating the site: continuous improvement

### Summary

- Don't stand still!
- Try to track your readership
- Obtain third party evaluations of your site

## You can't stand still

Since the internet environment doesn't stand still, nor can your site. Once you've finished the site, you must re-evaluate the site and plan the next generation:

- Benchmarking - how does it compare to other sites?

- What are its strengths and weaknesses?

- What impression does it convey?

- Are there good ideas from feedback?

- What's on your own wish list?

- Could it be more entertaining?

- Could it be more interactive?

- Could it generate more revenue?

To identify benchmark sites, go back to Step 1 and follow the suggestions for identifying your competitors' sites, best web sites and, also, in Step 12, award-winning web sites.

## Gathering feedback

Throughout the life of your website, use a spreadsheet to collate comments, ideas and suggestions as they are received. You will then have an extensive wish-list for use when the opportunity arises. Other feedback that you should gather includes:

- User 'comments on site' (there should be a box for clients to give this).

- Other comments made in e-mails, telephone enquiries or correspondence.

- Staff suggestions.

When you are planning further development, actively seek feedback from customers and other audiences on:

- their awareness of the site's existence;

- the frequency with which they visit the site;

- what they like or dislike on the site;

- new services or information that they would find helpful.

## How to track your site's visitors

The internet provides many opportunities for gaining intelligence about your customers, markets and competitors that you can use to plan and improve marketing activity, your website, and your products and services themselves.

### Hits, page impressions etc.

**Hits** are often quoted for websites, but are a misleading measure. Each page on a website is made up of a number of files, including graphics, HTML text etc. Each separate file counts as one 'hit' when the page is downloaded, so the more graphics you have, the more hits will be counted. This tells you nothing about the number of real visitors.

**Page views** count the number of times a page is downloaded. This provides a clearer view of use of your site.

### Counters

There are quite a few simple web visitor counters available free online. Check which one offers the features you need and fits your website best. Examples are www.thecounter.com, www.fastcounter.com or www.sitemeter.com. Visitor counts displayed on the home page itself were once popular but are now regarded as naff.

You can track how many times each of your links is clicked using www.linkcounter.com, also free. This can help you track which links within the site are used most and how much traffic you refer to other sites.

## Commercial software

For website statistics, www.webtrends.com is the most popular website statistics package, and as well as giving you numbers of hits and page impressions, it tells you the following about your visitors:

- How much time they spend on site.

- What time of day they use the site.

- Their top referring sites.

- Their top ten pages.

- Their country of origin.

These and similar packages will provide anonymous information which will not identify individual users.

## Cookies

Consider using 'cookies' that automatically capture data from visitors. Cookies are text files that your site can leave on a visitor's computer. Your site can then track an individual's progress through your site and recognise a repeat visitor. However, if you use cookies, you will need to explain this in your Privacy Policy, and you will need to allow users to withhold information in order to meet concerns about data protection and privacy. Visit www.cookiecentral.com for an example.

# Evaluation

Third party evaluations can be obtained: www.websitegarage.com remotely checks the logistics of your site. You can also monitor your site's availability using a service such as www.netwhistle.com and check for broken links, download time etc. with sites such as www.netmechanic.com.

Some web designers offer a 'web site workout' reviewing your site. Alternatively, free of charge, you can ask friends, relatives or colleagues to help. Ask them to:

- search for the site on the major internet search engine using your business name and relevant keywords;

- 'mystery shop' your email and interactive services to discover what response they receive, and how long it takes;

- look on your site for an item of information that you specify, and comment on how easy it was to locate it;

- comment on their instant reactions to the site, and what they liked or didn't like.

# Appendices

How to write effectively
The web and visually impaired users
Marketing plan checklist

# Appendix 1: How to write effectively

Whether you are writing a marketing email, an advertisement, content for your web site, a press release or other promotional material, your copy must grab attention, if the piece is to achieve your objectives.

## Plan effectively

- What is the goal of the piece?
- Who is the target audience?
- What will appeal to them?
- What is your key single selling point?

## Lead the reader to act

Cater for three stages through which readers will go:

1. **Scanning:** How will you catch the reader's attention and encourage them to want to know more?

2. **Review:** What explanatory information will you provide to keep the reader interested?

3. **Action:** What should readers do next to pursue their interest? Visit the web site, send an email, make a phone call? What are you offering in return for this commitment?

## Make headlines functional

- Make a positive statement.
- Avoid cute headlines which conceal their real meaning.

- Stimulate the reader to want to know more.

- Ask a question in the headline only if it will intrigue readers enough to want to continue.

## Write crisply

- Don't repeat the headline in the first line of text.

- Explain the key selling point at the beginning.

- Keep to one topic per paragraph.

- Avoid jargon - write in plain language.

## Draw the reader in

- Write about your readers: talk about 'you'.

- Use the active, not passive, voice.

- Sound positive.

## Make it easy to scan the text rapidly

- Keep paragraphs and sentences short.

- Break up longer pieces using sub-headings, bullet points, numbered lists, italicised or emboldened text.

- Don't overuse capitals: lower case is easier to read.

## Gain and keep attention

- Appeal to the reader's self-interest or anxieties.

- Offer real benefits.

- Emphasise the unexpected, unique or new.

## Don't oversell

- Think and write from the buyer's perspective - not your own.

- Don't oversell your product or your company.

- If you have any evidence about the benefits you claim, provide it.

## Remember other points

- Beware of race, gender or age bias or assumptions. Apart from legal risks, you will immediately alienate important sections of your audience.

- Take care with humour - jokes are not always universally funny.

- Check all spelling - remember that computerised spellchecker and grammar checkers may not catch every mistake.

- Double-check telephone, fax and email details and spellings of named companies and individuals.

See also...

- Tips on writing a press release - see page 116.

- Guidelines for preparing a web site banner advertising campaign - see page 113.

# Appendix 2: The web and visually impaired users

## How to find out more

If you are rebuilding or extending your web presence, why not make use of the free practical guides to help ensure accessible design? Online resources include the following:

- Guides at www.rnib.org.uk/digital and www.w3.org/WAI (site of the Web Access Initiative), the British Computer Society at www.bcs.org.uk and, finally, www.ability.co.uk.

- At www.cast.org/bobby, you can test your site for compliance with accessibility standards.

- The Employers' Forum on Disability at www.employers-forum.co.uk has published the *Accessible Website Guide* with both practical step-by-step guidance and technical advice.

- At www.guidedogs.org.uk you'll find a web site designed for visually impaired users, and you'll see it's as attractive and effective as any other. Incidentally, it includes simulations to show what people with different impairments can see.

## Why it's worth addressing the needs of visually impaired users

The growth of the World Wide Web has meant that many people with serious sight problems are now able to enjoy a wealth of information that was previously unavailable to them. With the help of synthesised speech and braille display technology, even completely blind people can use the internet.

However, for these technologies to work properly, web pages must be written in correct HTML (hypertext mark-up language).

Most people with sight problems have some useful vision, and read online text in exactly the same way as fully sighted people: with their eyes. However, the needs of people with poor sight vary, depending on how their eye condition affects their vision.

Some people require large text, while others can only read smaller letters. Most people need a highly contrasting colour scheme, while some can only read yellow text on a black background. To cater for everyone, web sites should be flexible in design, enabling the individual to adjust the text and colour settings to suit their needs and circumstances.

In contrast, people with very little or no vision read web pages with the help of access technology installed on their computer. Synthesised speech software reads the content of web pages aloud through a speaker, while braille software outputs to a retractable display, so that the web site can be read by touch. Careful design is paramount for people accessing the web in these ways, as inappropriate use of HTML can render a site unreadable.

An accessible web site is one that can be visited by anybody. It is perfectly possible to produce an attractive, dynamic design that remains fully accessible. Websites that are designed intelligently benefit everyone - not only people with disabilities.

## The RNIB's ten tips

1.   **Is the text legible?**

Contrast is the most important factor to consider when designing sites that everyone can use. Go for text and background colour combinations that offer maximum contrast.

2.   **Is the design flexible?**

Is it easy to change the colours and the size of the text by adjusting browser settings?

3.   **Does every image have 'alt-text'?**

The alternative text attribute of the image tag exists to provide a description of the image for people accessing the site via speech synthesis software.

4.   **Is there a site map?**

A site map will help visitors to get an impression of the layout of the site quickly and will make it easier to navigate.

5.   **Do links make sense out of context?**

Sighted people scan screens of information to locate the parts that interest them. If you cannot see, and rely on synthesised speech technology to 'hear' web sites, you need another way to get a quick impression of the content of a page. Commonly, the access software blind people use will provide a list of all the links on a page as a means of getting the 'flavour' of the content. If a link contains only the words 'click here', its function will not be obvious if it is presented out of context.

6. **Are imagemaps accompanied by text links?**

Some of the software packages that blind people use cannot read imagemaps, so it is important to make text links available as well.

7. **Do frames have titles, or is 'noframes' used?**

Some blind people may be using software that cannot read frames. It is vital that the NOFRAMES tag is used to offer these people alternative frames-free versions of your pages.

8. **Are alternatives offered for JavaScript, applets, Flash or plug-ins?**

If you are writing pages in anything other than HTML, you may be excluding some people from your site.

9. **Is Access Adobe available for PDF files?**

Adobe Acrobat Reader is not compatible with the access software many blind people use. Access Adobe transforms PDF files into HTML.

10. **Do all pages pass the 'Bobby' test?**

The Centre for Applied Special Technology (CAST) has created an automated accessibility checker, code-named Bobby. Bobby will test for HTML 4.0 compatibility, that all graphic elements have text equivalents, and that written summaries have been provided for graphs and statistical material.

**Julie Howell**

Campaigns Officer (Access to Digital Information), RNIB

*Reproduced from the London Advice Service Alliance site*

*www.lasa.org.uk/knowledgebase*

# Appendix 3: Marketing plan checklist

## 1: Where are we now?

- The market
- Competition
- Our environment
- The business
- Market research
- Marketing activity to date
- Web site statistics and feedback
- SWOT analysis

## 2: Where do we want to be?

- Our overall business goals
- Our goals for the internet
- Our 'brand' and replicating it online
- Marketing goals for our web site

## 3: Our audience

- Our target markets
- Research data on their characteristics

## 4: How will we get there?

- Objectives (model objectives are included - see page 34)
- Table showing:

  - objective;

  - action needed to achieve it;

  - how progress will be measured.

## 5: Plan for web site content and services

- Free content and services

- Paid-for content and services

- Interactive services

- E-commerce

- 'Virtual' services

- Extranet

## 6: People

- The project team

- Staff training

- Internet administrator's job specification

- Internal launch

## 7: Web designer

- Selection and appointment

- Preparation of Invitation to Tender and contract

## 8: Domain name

- Registration of sub-domains
- Plans for .biz and .info protective registrations

## 9: Technology

- Requirements of 'frames' and 'plug-ins' to be written into the web site designer's Invitation to Tender
- Security: Hardware and software requirements
- E-commerce systems
- Marketing database
- Future-proofing

## 10: Outline design brief

- Look and feel
- Navigation
- Catering for visually impaired users (see Appendix 2, page 140)
- (See also guide to effective writing in Appendix 1, page 137)

## 11: Risk management

- Site testing
- Arrangements for monitoring the site
- Checking compliance on legal issues such as Data Protection and Distance Selling

- Evaluation of our ecommerce capability

## 12: Promotion activity

- Offline marketing: Press launch and direct mail
- Email campaign
- Visits to newsgroups and chatrooms
- Mutual links with other web sites
- Online advertising
- Online directories
- Customer incentives
- Online press relations activity (includes guidelines for writing press releases - see page 116)
- Entering the site for competitions and awards
- Metatags etc.
- Submitting our pages to search-engines regularly

## 13: Updating the site

- Resources for updating
- Schedule for updates

## 14: Monitoring, evaluation, future development

- Statistical reports from the site
- Post-launch review
- Market research

# Index

## A

accessibility *see* visually impaired users
address lists  81, 108
administration systems, own  60–1, 63, 66
Adobe Acrobat  80
advertisements
 banners
  agreements  114
  exchange services  115
  limitations  111–13
  prices  113
  research  113
 in directories  114–15
 in email newsletters  110
 limitations  40–1
 in other sites  110
 pop-ups  111
algorithms  120
animation  80–1
arbitration, names, choosing  77
ASP database systems  120
assessment
 of other businesses *see* market
 research
 of own business  4
  audits  18
  reviews, formal  17
  SWOT analysis  19–20
audio-visual software  81
audits
 of internet  20
 of own business  18

awards  117–19

## B

B2B (business-to-business) users  30
B2C (business-to-consumer) users  30
back office systems  82
banners
 agreements  114
 exchange services  115
 limitations  111–13
 prices  113
 research  113
benchmarking  11–12, 18, 20, 130 *see also*
  passive marketing
benefits
 business  45
 customers'  12, 28, 44–6, 89
  copy on 138–9
bespoke systems  56, 83–4
brands
 consistency in  25–6
 core qualities  24
 criticisms  76–7, 104
 images as  23–4, 26
 invisible identities  25
 names as *see* names
 on prices  40
 visible identities  24–5
brochure sites  44
bulletin boards  52
Business Links  61
business-to-business (B2B) users  30

business-to-consumer (B2C) users 30

# C

C2B (consumer-to-business) users 30
calculations, using email 49–50
cannibalisation 40, 58–9, 101 *see also* channel conflicts
ccTLDs (country-code Top Level Domains) 71
CGI database systems 120
channel conflicts 41, 58–9, 101 *see also* cannibalisation
Chartered Institute of Marketing 7
chatrooms 51, 52, 109, 110
checklists 143–6
    for visually impaired users 141–2
competitions 117–18
competitiveness 22
complaints
    by email 49
    orders 55–6
consistency, in brands 25–6
consultancy 63, 64, 66
Consumer Protection (Distance Selling) Regulations 2000 100
consumer-to-business (C2B) users 30
consumer-to-consumer (P2P) users 30
content 39–40
    additional 41, 44–6, 47
    basic 44
    email 106
        press releases by 116–17
    free 8–10, 79
        limitations 40
    scope 46
    tests on 96
contracts, sites
    development 68
    maintenance 68–9

cookies 55, 99, 108, 132 *see also* privacy
'cool' sites 11
copy 60–1
    clarity 138
    on customers' benefits 138–9
    directed 137
    in emails 106
    headlines 137–8
    inclusion in 139
    interest 137
    persuasion 138
    press releases, by email 116, 117
    proofreading 139
    succinctness 138
    underselling 139
    *see also* designers; offline marketing
copyright, illustrations 91
counters, of users 131–2 *see also* tracking services
country-code Top Level Domains (ccTLDs) 71
credit card systems 84
currency 10
    updates 129
    visibility 129
customers 25
    catering to needs 12, 28, 44–6, 89
        copy on 138–9
    choosing 28
    communication 23, 26–7 *see also* email
    criticisms by 76–7, 104
    deliveries by 102
    difficult to please 88
    extranet access 56
    orders *see* orders
    points system incentives 115–16
    in relationship vs transactional marketing 42–3
    types 30

*see also* visitors
cybersquatting  72, 76

# D

data protection  99, 107–8
Data Protection Acts 1994, 1998  99
databases  99, 107–8
    basic  81–2
    from cookies  108
    in-depth  82
    scope  81
    systems  120
decision-trees  50
definitions
    ecommerce  52
    marketing  6, 103
deliveries
    by customers  102
    details  56
    unreliability  101–2
delivery channels  85–6
designers  64
    choosing  66–7
    contracts  68–9
    questions to  65–6
    tenders  67–8
    *see also* copy; offline marketing
directories, advertisements in  114–15
distance selling regulations
    requirements  100
    scope  99–100
domain names *see* names
doorway pages  121

# E

email  48
    address lists  81, 108

advantages  104–5
calculations using  49–50
communication from  106
content  106
copy  106
feedback by  49
immediacy  49
information  106
junk mail  106–7
limitations  106–7
press releases by
    content  116–17
    copy  116, 117
    information  116
response times  107
viral marketing by  105
*see also* customers, communication
email newsletters, advertisements in  110
efficiency  23
extranets  56

# F

feedback  130–1
    by email  49
Flash 5  80–1
frames
    advantages  84
    disadvantages  84–5
free content  8–10, 79
    limitations  40
future
    advances  12–13
    email *see* email
    goals *see* goals
    iTV  85–6
    limitations  32
    mobile internet  87
    objectives *see* objectives

text messaging 86–7

### G

generic Top Level Domains (gTLDs) 70–1
goals 4
    brands 23–6
    competitiveness 22
    customers, communication 23, 26–7
    efficiency as 23
    overview 21–2
    USPs 22–3, 27
    *see also* objectives
golden rules 4
gTLDs (generic Top Level Domains) 70–1

### H

headlines 137–8
hits 131
Home Pages
    clarity 90
    illustrations 90–2
    publishing styles 88–9
    user-friendly 88, 89
homes, internet use at, vs work use 31
hosting 66 *see also* support systems, external
    contracts 68–9
HTML (hypertext mark-up language) 120–1

### I

ICANN (Internet Corporation for Assigned Names and Numbers) 70, 72
illustrations 90
    appearance 91–2
    copyright 91
    speeding up 91

images 23–4, 26
inclusion
    in copy 139
    visually impaired *see* visually impaired users
increases, users 30–1
integration 40, 58–9, 102
Internet Corporation for Assigned Names and Numbers (ICANN) 70, 72
invisibility, in brands 25
iTV
    advantages 85, 86
    limitations 85, 86

### J

Javascript 80
junk mail 106–7

### K

key principles 4–5
keywords 121, 122

### L

legal compliance
    information 97–8
    local jurisdiction 98
life-cycles, products 32–3
links
    advantages 47
    limitations 46–7, 98
    mutual 115

### M

maintenance, external 66 *see also* support

systems, external
  contracts 68–9
market leaders 11–12, 127–8
  case studies 53
  search engines as 124
market research 5
  benchmarking 11–12, 18, 20, 130
  cost-effective strategies 18–19
  information
    about marketing 7–8
    about the internet 8–12
  passive marketing 104
metatags 121–2, 123
mobile phones
  internet 87
  text messaging 86–7
mouse-overs 81

## N

names 7
  checking 71
  choosing
    arbitration 77
    clarity 73
    existing 75
    existing endings 71
    generic terms 74
    new 74–5
    new endings 71–2
    non-roman characters 75
    unofficial endings 73
  criticisms 76–7, 104
  cybersquatting 72, 76
  invisible identity 70
  levels 70–1
  multiple 75–6
  ownership 76
  registration 71, 72, 101

  trademarks 77–8
  shortcuts to 75
navigation aids
  clarity 92
  information in 92–3
netiquette 106–7
NewNet 73
newsgroups 109, 110

## O

objectives 5
  planning 34
    SMART 34–5
  specified 35
  see also goals
off-the-shelf systems 56–7, 83–4
  information 64–5
offline marketing 103–4 see also copy; designers
opinion-formers 29
opt-in/opt-out boxes 108
orders 50
  ability to fulfil 101–2
  complaints 55–6
  credit card systems 84
  delivery details 56
  from distance selling 99–100
  information with 54
    clarity 55
  privacy 54–5, 56
  secure sites 55
  tracking services 52
  user-friendly 54
ownership
  names 76
  sites 65
  staff involvement as see staff

# P

P2P (consumer-to-consumer) users  30
page views  131
passive marketing  104 *see also* benchmarking
plug-ins  80–1
points system incentives  115–16
pop-ups  80
    advertisements  111
press releases, by email
    content  116–17
    copy  116, 117
    information  116
prices
    advertisements, limitations  40–1
    banner advertisements  113
    brands on  40
    clarity  54
    conflict factors  40, 41, 58–9, 101
    for content  40
PRINCE (Projects In Controlled
Environments)  59–60
privacy  54–5, 56
    data protection  99, 107–8
    databases  81–2, 99, 107, 108, 120
    opt-in/opt-out boxes  108
    *see also* cookies
products  4
    conflict factors  41
    failing  53
    life-cycles  32–3
    orders *see* orders
    successful  52–3
    suppliers  29
project teams  59–60
Projects In Controlled Environments
(PRINCE)  59–60
Ps, the six  6–7

# Q

questions, to designers  65–6

# R

recruitment, staff  29
referrals  29
registration
    names  71, 72, 101
    search engines
        automated  126–7
        content  124–5
        waiting times  125–6
    users  50, 108
relationship marketing
    email *see* email
    interaction  48
        bulletin boards  52
        chatrooms  51, 52, 109, 110
    vs transaction marketing  42–3
reviews, formal, of own business  17
RNIB (Royal National Institute for the Blind),
          checklist  141–2

# S

search engines  66
    algorithms  120
    database systems  120
    doorway pages  121
    graphics  123
    HTML  120–1
    keywords  121, 122
    market leaders  124
    metatags and  121–2, 123
    prominence in  119
    promotions by, charges  127
    registration

automated 126–7
content 124–5
waiting times 125–6
submission policies 125
types 119–20
second level domains 71
security
orders 55
policies 83
sites 55
systems 82–3
self-employed users 31
services *see* products
silver surfers 31
small to medium enterprises (SMEs) 42
SMART objectives 34–5
SMEs (small to medium enterprises) 42
spamming 106–7
staff 29
integration 58–9
project teams 59–60
recruitment 29
resistance by, positive responses to
61–2, 63
responsibilities 60
roles 60–1
skills 60
support systems 60–1, 63, 66
statistics packages 132
submission policies, search engines 125
suppliers, products 29
support systems
external 63, 64, 66, 68–9
internal 60–1, 63, 66
by staff *see* staff
SWOT analysis 19–20

**T**

television 85–6

tenders, designers 67–8
tests
on content 96
functions 97
by users 133
by web sites 132–3
text, hidden 81
text messaging 86–7
tracking services 52 *see also* counters, of users
trademarks, names 77–8
training, information on 8, 9–10
transaction marketing, vs relationship
marketing 42–3
trends
advances 12–13, 41–2
advantages 21
market leaders 11–12, 53,
127–8
successful products 52–3
email *see* email
goals *see* goals
iTV 85–6
limitations 13, 41, 42, 52
advertisements 111–13
failing products 53
mobile internet 87
objectives *see* objectives
text messaging 86–7

**U**

unique selling points (USPs) 22–3, 27
unreliability, deliveries 101–2
USPs (unique selling points) 22–3, 27

**V**

viral marketing 105
virtual businesses 57

visibility  3
        in brands  24–5
        in currency  129
visitors  29
        registration  50, 108
        self-employed users  31
        silver surfers  31
        tracking  55, 99, 108, 131–2
        types  30
        visually impaired *see* visually
impaired users
        *see also* customers
visually impaired users  79, 93–4
        aids  141
        checklists  141–2
        information  140

# W

WIPO (World Internet Property
        Organisation)  77
work, internet use at, vs home use  31
World Internet Property Organisation
        (WIPO)  77

# More books available from Law Pack...

## How to Make Money Online

Forget the high-profile dot com failures - there are businesses out there making money online. This guide includes what will and won't sell, how to avoid e-business mistakes, how to give web site visitors the confidence to buy online, getting payments, security software and systems, digital certificates and e-signatures, selling advertising space, supplying content, and much more!

| Code B604 | ISBN 1 902646 76 2 | PB |
|---|---|---|
| 250 x 199mm | 160pp | £9.99 | Jan 2002 |

## The Legal Guide to Online Business

Going online opens up a world of legal issues that can't be ignored. Domain names, trade marks, international jurisdictions, credit card transactions, partnerships, alliances, online contracts, employee email and internet policies and cyber crimes are some of the issues discussed and explained by specialist solicitor, Susan Singleton. Template documents included.

| Code B603 | ISBN 1 902646 77 0 | PB |
|---|---|---|
| 250 x 199mm | 160pp | £9.99 | Nov 2001 |

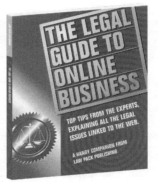

## Secrets of Successful Websites

Some web sites get it right, many get it wrong. This guide divulges what makes a successful site. It covers identifying the audience and their needs, choosing the right model for your site, choosing the right technology and ISP, getting the best help with implementation, design and branding, risk management and testing procedures.

| Code B601 | ISBN 1 902646 74 6 | PB |
|---|---|---|
| 250 x 199mm | 160pp | £9.99 | Jan 2002 |

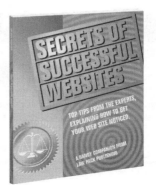

To order, visit www.lawpack.co.uk or call 020 7940 7000

## More books available from Law Pack...

### Limited Company Formation

Incorporation as a limited liability company is the preferred structure for thousands of successful businesses. *Limited Company Formation Made Easy* Guide explains why, and shows you how to set up your own limited liability company easily and inexpensively. It provides detailed but easy to follow instructions, background information, completed examples of Companies House forms and drafts of other necessary documents.

| Code B503 | ISBN 1 902646 43 6 | | PB | |
|---|---|---|---|---|
| 250 x 199mm | 112pp | £9.99 | 1st edition | |

### Profitable Mail-Order

Mail-order business is big business, and it's growing year by year. Setting up and running your own mail-order business can be fun as well as profitable. This *Made Easy* Guide shows you how to do it, explaining the vital importance of product profile, building valuable mailing lists, effective advertising and a whole lot more. It divulges the mail-order secrets that ensure success!

| Code B510 | ISBN 1 902646 46 0 | | PB | |
|---|---|---|---|---|
| 250 x 199mm | 206pp | £9.99 | 1st edition | |

### Running Your Own Business

You have a business idea that you want to put into action, but you also want advice on the realities of setting up and running a business: this *Made Easy* Guide is for you. It takes you through the business-creation process, from assessing your aptitude and ideas, to funding and business plans.

| Code B511 | ISBN 1 902646 47 9 | | PB | |
|---|---|---|---|---|
| 250 x 199mm | 140pp | £9.99 | 1st edition | |

To order, visit www.lawpack.co.uk or call 020 7940 7000